D1446642

*Studies in the Vocabulary of the
Greek New Testament*

WORD STUDIES IN
THE GREEK NEW TESTAMENT
For the English Reader

by Kenneth S. Wuest

1. GOLDEN NUGGETS FROM THE GREEK N. T.
2. BYPATHS IN THE GREEK N. T.
3. TREASURES FROM THE GREEK N. T.
4. UNTRANSLATABLE RICHES
5. PHILIPPIANS
6. FIRST PETER
7. GALATIANS
8. STUDIES IN VOCABULARY
9. HEBREWS
10. MARK
11. GREAT TRUTHS TO LIVE BY
12. THE PASTORIAL EPISTLES
13. EPHESIANS AND COLOSSIANS
14. IN THESE LAST DAYS
15. PROPHETIC LIGHT IN THE PRESENT DARKNESS
16. ROMANS

Also by Kenneth S. Wuest

THE NEW TESTAMENT
IN EXPANDED TRANSLATION

Studies in the Vocabulary
of the
Greek New Testament

FOR THE ENGLISH READER

by

Kenneth S. Wuest

WM. B. EERDMANS PUBLISHING COMPANY

Grand Rapids   Michigan

STUDIES IN THE VOCABULARY OF THE GREEK NEW TESTAMENT
FOR THE ENGLISH READER
by Kenneth S. Wuest

Copyright 1945, *by*
Wm. B. Eerdmans Publishing Company

Set up and printed, 1945
Tenth printing, August 1974

ISBN 0-8028-1240-6

PHOTOLITHOPRINTED BY GRAND RAPIDS BOOK MANUFACTURERS, INC.
GRAND RAPIDS, MICHIGAN

DEDICATED

To Richard W. Oliver, who is now in the presence
of his Lord, and Howard W. Ferrin, classmates of
mine who, during student days at Northwestern
University, instructed me in the Word, and directed
me to The Moody Bible Institute for training in
Christian service—for which I shall ever be
grateful.

Preface

One who undertakes to study God's Word and to explain it to others, should be a student of words. To the extent that he understands the meaning of the words in the New Testament, to that extent is he able to understand its statements and make them clear to others.

While the words used in the English New Testament are for the most part simple and easy to understand, yet there are factors involved which make a knowledge of the Greek words very helpful in arriving at an accurate, full-orbed interpretation of the passage in question.

For instance, some English words have changed their meaning in the 300 years since the Authorized Version was translated. Since this version still remains the most widely used translation of the Scriptures, there is need of bringing that particular part of the translation up to date. Then again, a student of the English Bible often interprets a word according to its current usage in ordinary conversation instead of in its more specialized meaning. Again, in the case of synonyms, one English word may be the translation of four Greek words, each having a shade of meaning slightly different from the other. This added light is denied the student of the English Bible. Consequently, while he may not arrive at an erroneous interpretation of the passage where the particular word occurs, yet he does not have as accurate and clear an interpretation of it as he might have. Or again, a Greek word may have a very rich content of meaning which would demand a few sentences if not a paragraph to bring out. But in a translation like the A.V., where the translation is held down to a minimum of words, it is impossible to bring out this richness of meaning. A knowledge of the Greek word is of help here.

Then, there are some words dealing with the theology of the N.T., or its doctrines, which are not understood by the English reader, but where a knowledge of the Greek word and its usage is of great help.

The purpose of this book is to make available to the Bible student who does not know Greek, an English-Greek vocabulary of some of the words used in the New Testament. The plan has been to give the English word, the Greek word of which it is the translation, in transliterated form, the various meanings of the Greek word, and where necessary, every place where the Greek word is found in the New Testament. The student of the English Bible can therefore obtain a clearer, more comprehensive view of the English word he is studying, by understanding the Greek word of which it is the translation.

Where no concordance is given of a word, the student should understand that the English word is in its every occurrence, the uniform translation of the Greek word. Where a concordance is given, the reason for the same may be that various English words are used to translate the one Greek word, the variants being given in each case. Or, in the case of synonyms, a concordance is necessary, since two or more Greek words are translated by the one English word. Again, a concordance is given at times so that the student can make a study of the word in its every occurrence in the New Testament. There are a few words that are treated only in particular passages, where the definitions of the Greek word will not hold in other places where this English word is used, and for the reason that other Greek words are found in the text. These will be marked "Limited."

The author, in defining the Greek word, has tried to give a well-rounded and complete view of it. The classical usage is presented first, next, the Koine usage in secular documents, and then the New Testament usage. Before 332 B.C., Greek was confined for the most part to Greece itself. The term "classical" is used to speak of Greek as it was spoken by the Greeks themselves in their own country prior to this date. But when Alexander the Great conquered the Medo-Persian empire, his armies spread the knowledge of the Greek language over the then-known world. Remaining as armies of occupation, and settling amongst the conquered peoples, they popularized the language, simplifying its grammatical and syntactical structure. The language as spoken by them became what is called Koine Greek. The word Koine means "common," and refers to the fact that the mingling of the various Greek tribes and dialects in the great armies of Greece, produced a common language, a language held in common by all Greeks, whereas before, the country of Greece was divided into various Greek states, each having its own Greek dialect. This Greek is called Koine. This is the Greek that became the international language.

Classical Greek compared to Koine Greek is comparable to English used by the great writers of the past as the latter is compared to the English which the average person uses in ordinary conversation. The Greek translation of the Old Testament, the Septuagint, is in Koine Greek. The New Testament is written in the same style of Greek. The New Testament was therefore written in the language of the ordinary person, not in the language of the scholar.

The author has not only tried to give the reader a view of the word as it was used by the ancient Greeks, but also a conception of how it was used by the average person in the first century in his ordinary conversation. In addition to that, he has presented the usage of the word in the New Testament.

Thus, after the student has examined all the various uses of the word, he can form a better, more accurate, and full-orbed conception of that word. Of course, he will not use the purely classical meaning of the word when interpreting the New Testament, except where the author has indicated, or where the context clearly shows that the purely classical meaning is used. The classical meaning is given so that the student may have some background against which he can obtain a better appreciation of the word as it is used in the New Testament.

The student should first set before himself the goal of studying and mastering the meanings of each word. He can then use the book as a reference work when studying the New Testament. He can either start at the beginning and work slowly through the book, or he can consult the index, choose the particular word that suits his fancy, and check the word off after he has studied it. A study of a single word would mean that the student gain a comprehensive view of the Greek word, and then study the passages in which it occurs. That will give him a bird's-eye view of the word as it is used in the New Testament. In case a concordance of the word is not given, the student should consult a Cruden's Concordance.

The reader is cautioned against putting this book on the shelf as a reference work merely. If he does that, he will deprive himself of a great deal of valuable information that would stand him in good stead in his study of the New Testament. If he puts himself to the discipline of working through this book, he will have gained not only a more accurate knowledge of these New Testament words, but also much spiritual truth. *This book is more than an English-Greek vocabulary. It offers an intensive study of the words it treats as they are related to their context in the New Testament. Furthermore, the study of these words in their every occurrence in the New Testament, will open up many new lines of truth, and afford a new and clearer appreciation of the passages studied. Pastors and other Christian workers will obtain fresh material and new ideas for Bible messages.*

The English translation used is the Authorized Version. The Greek authorities quoted are: Joseph H. Thayer, *Greek-English Lexicon of the New Testament;* Liddel and Scott, *Greek-English Lexicon* (classical) ; Archbishop Trench, *Syno-*

nyms of the New Testament; Marvin R. Vincent, *Word Studies in the New Testament;* Herman Cremer, *Biblico-Theological Lexicon of New Testament Greek;* James Hope Moulton and George Milligan, *Vocabulary of the Greek Testament,* the work of these scholars being based upon the papyri, the latter being contemporary secular documents written in Koine Greek.   **K. S. W.**

ARCHBISHOP TRENCH,

On the Study of Synonyms

"The value of this study as a discipline for training the mind into close and accurate habits of thought, the amount of instruction which may be drawn from it, the increase of intellectual wealth which it may yield, all this has been implicitly recognized by well-nigh all great writers — for well-nigh all from time to time have paused, themselves to play the dividers and discerners of words — explicitly by not a few who have proclaimed the value which this study had in their eyes. And instructive as in any language it must be, it must be eminently so in the Greek — a language spoken by a people of the subtlest intellect; who saw distinctions, where others saw none; who divided out to different words what others often were content to huddle confusedly under a common term; who were themselves singularly alive to its value, diligently cultivating the art of synonymous distinction . . .; and who have bequeathed a multitude of fine and delicate observations on the right discrimination of their own words to the after world. . . .

"And while thus the characteristic excellences of the Greek language especially invite us to the investigation of the likenesses and differences between words, to the study of the words of the New Testament there are reasons additional inviting us. If by such investigations as these we become aware of delicate variations in an author's meaning, which otherwise we might have missed, where is it so desirable that we should miss nothing, that we should lose no finer intention of the writer, as in those words which are the vehicles of the very mind of God Himself? If thus the intellectual riches of the student

15

are increased, can this anywhere be of so great importance as there, where the intellectual may, if rightly used, prove spiritual riches as well? If it encourage thoughtful meditation on the exact forces of words, both as they are in themselves, and in their relation to other words, or in any way unveil to us their marvel and their mystery, this can nowhere else have a worth in the least approaching that which it acquires when the words with which we have to do are, to those who receive them aright, words of eternal life; while in the dead carcasses of the same, if men suffer the spirit of life to depart from them, all manner of corruptions and heresies may be, as they have been, bred.

"The *words* of the New Testament are eminently the *stoicheia* (rudiments, elements) of Christian theology, and he who will not begin with a patient study of those, shall never make any considerable, least of all any secure, advances in this: for here, as everywhere else, sure disappointment awaits him who thinks to possess the whole without first possessing the parts of which that whole is composed."[1]

------

1. *Synonyms of the New Testament, R. C. Trench.*

VOCABULARY

A

	Page
Abide[1]	64
Access	79
Accounted	84
Admonition	115
Adoption	77
Air	76
Another	142

B

Baptism	70
Baptize	70
Beast	45
Believe	28
Blessed	22
Bowels	43

C

Chastening	115
Choose	34
Church	27
Comfort	80
Comforter	82
Coming[2]	65
Communion	33
Confess	41
Conform	52
Conversation	66
Counted	84

D

	Page
Disciple	25
Disorderly	25
Dwell[3]	63

E

Empty	139
Envy	110

F

Faith	28
Faithfulness	28
Fellowship	33
Fight	148
Foreknowledge	34
Form	49
Forsaken	47

G

Gentleness	107
Godhead	53
Gospel	42
Grace	132

H

Hallow	80
Harpazo	68
Hebrew	127
Hell	48
Holy	30
Humility	100

1, 2, 3. *Limited*

Page

I

Imputed 84
Israelite 127

J

Jew 127
Justify 36

M

Meekness 105
Mercy 132

P

Parable 27
Perfect 21
Predestinate 33
Prophecy 123
Propitiation 38

Q

Quick 69
Quicken 69

R

Reckon 84
Regeneration 89
Renewing 89

Page

Repent 27
Rest 113
Righteousness 36

S

Saint 30
Sanctify 30
Servant 117
Sin 95
Synagogue 27

T

Temple 46
Trance 82
Transfigure 51
Transform 52
True 86
Truth 86

V

Vain 139
Vile[4] 64

W

Word 60
World 55

4. *Limitea*

*Studies in the Vocabulary of the
Greek New Testament*

Studies in the Vocabulary of the Greek New Testament

PERFECT. There are four words translated by the one word *perfect*. These must be distinguished.

Telaios the adjective, and *teleioo* the verb. The adjective is used in the papyri, of heirs being of age, of women who have attained maturity, of full-grown cocks, of acacia trees in good condition, of a complete lampstand, of something in good working order or condition. To summarize; the meaning of the adjective includes the ideas of full-growth, maturity, workability, soundness, and completeness. The verb refers to the act of bringing the person or thing to any one of the aforementioned conditions. When applied to a Christian, the word refers to one that is spiritually mature, complete, well-rounded in his Christian character.

The word occurs in the following scriptures; the adjective and noun in *Mt.* 5:48, 19:21; *Lk.* 1:45 (performance); *Rom.* 12:2; I *Cor.* 2:6, 13:10, 14:20 (*men*); *Eph.* 4:13; *Phil.* 3:15; *Col.* 1:28, 3:14, 4:12; *Heb.* 5:14 (of full age), 7:11, 9:11; *Jas.* 1:4, 17, 25, 3:2; I *John* 4:18; *Col.* 3:14; *Heb.* 6:1, 12:2 (finisher); I *Pet.* 1:13 (to the end); the verb in *Lk.* 2:43 (*had fulfilled*) 13:32; *John* 4:34 (*finish*), 5:36 (*finish*), 17:4, (*have finished*) 17:23, 19:28 (*fulfilled*); *Acts* 20:24 (*finish*); II *Cor.* 7:1, 12:9; *Gal.* 3:3; *Phil.* 3:12; *Heb.* 2:10, 5:9, 7:19, 28 (*consecrated*), 9:9, 10:1, 14, 11:40, 12:23; *Jas.* 2:22; I *John* 2:5, 4:12, 17, 18. Study these passages in the light of the above definitions, select the one that agrees best with the context, and see what additional light is thrown upon the passage, and how much clearer it becomes.

Katartizo. This word has the following meanings: "to repair, to restore to a former good condition, to prepare, to fit out, to equip." It was used of reconciling factions, setting broken bones, putting a dislocated limb into place, mending nets. Paul used it metaphorically in the sense of setting a person to rights, of bringing him into line. Used of a Christian, it referred to his equipment for Christian service (Eph. 4:11, 12). The verb occurs in *Mt.* 4:21 (*mending*), 21:16; *Mk.* 1:19; *Lk.* 6:40, *Rom.* 9:22 (*fitted*); *I Cor.* 1:10 (*perfectly joined together*), *II Cor.* 13:11; *Gal.* 6:1 (*restore*); *I Thes.* 3:10; *Heb.* 10:5 (*prepared*), 11:3 (*framed*), 13:21; *I Pet.* 5:10; the noun in *II Cor.* 13:9; *Eph.* 4:12.

In contrasting these two words, we would say that *teleios* refers to Christian experience, *katartizo* to Christian service, *teleios* to maturity and completeness of Christian character, *katartizo* to equipment for service.

Akribes, meaning "exactly, accurately, diligently," is translated by the word *perfect* in *Acts* 18:26, 23:15, 20, 24:22. In *II Tim.* 3:17, *perfect* is from *artios,* meaning "fitted, complete."

BLESSED. There are two Greek words, each with its distinctive meaning, both translated by the one word *blessed.*

Makarios. Some classical writers used this word to describe the state of the Greek gods as distinct from that of men who were subject to poverty and death, denoting a state of being of the gods who were exalted above earthly suffering and the limitations of earthly life. It was also used of the dead. Another word, *eudaimon,* was used of human happiness. Other writers used *makarios* to describe the state of certain men as supremely blest, fortunate, prosperous, wealthy. *Makarios* was chosen by the Bible writers to describe the state of the man who is the recipient of the divine favor and blessing. The LXX[5] uses it in Psalm 1:1, "Oh, the happiness of,"

---

5. *The Greek translation of the Old Testament.*

where it is the Greek translation of a word that in Hebrew thought denotes a state of true well-being. Cremer says that "it is the gracious and saving effect of God's favor . . ., but is enjoyed only when there is a corresponding behavior towards God; so that it forms the hoped-for good of those who in this life are subject to oppression." He says that, "In the N.T., *makarios* is quite a religiously qualified conception, expressing the life-joy and satisfaction of the man who does or shall experience God's favor and salvation, his blessedness altogether apart from his outward condition . . . It always signifies a happiness produced by some experience of God's favor, and specially conditioned by the revelation of grace." In summing up the meaning of the word as used of the state or condition of the believer, we would say that it refers to the spiritually prosperous state of that person who is the recipient of the sanctifying work of the Holy Spirit, who is enabled to minister these blessings to him when the believer yields to Him for that ministry and cooperates with Him in it. For instance, those who are reproached for the name of Christ, are in a spiritually prosperous condition, for the Holy Spirit is ministering to them with refreshing power (I Peter 4:14). Or, "Spiritually prosperous are the meek, for they shall inherit the earth" (Mt. 5:5). See classical usage of *makarios* (fortunate) in Acts 26:2, also in I Tim. 1:11, 6:15 (the state of exaltation above humanity). The word occurs in *Mt.* 5:3-11, 11:6, 13:16, 16:17, 24:46; *Lk.* 1:45, 6:20, 21, 22, 7:23, 10:23, 11:27, 28, 12:37, 38, 43, 14:14, 15, 23:29; *John* 13:17 (*happy*), 20:29; *Acts* 20:35, 26:2 (*happy*); *Rom.* 4:7, 8, 14:22 (*happy*); *I Cor.* 7:40 (*happier*); *I Tim.* 1:11, 6:15; *Tit.* 2:13; *Jas.* 1:12, 25; *I Pet.* 3:14 (*happy*), 4:14 (*happy*); Rev. 1:3, 14:13, 16:15, 19:9, 20:6, 22:7, 14. The noun *makarismos* is found in *Rom.* 4:6, 9; *Gal.* 4:15.

Eulogeo the verb, *eulogetos* the adjective, and *eulogia*, the noun. In classical Greek, *eulogeo* meant "to speak well of, to praise." *Eulogia* meant "good speaking, good words." The word is a compound of *eu* meaning "well, good" and *logeo* related to *lego,* "to speak." Our words "eulogy" and "eulogize" are derived from this Greek word. It was used in the pagan religions, as when a person who was chastened for his sin by the god, dedicates a monument to the god, and in doing so *eulogeo,* speaks well of, praises the deity. An extract from the Christian papyri gives us, "to the beloved brother who is also well-spoken of."[6] *Eulogia* is used in the same literature in the sense of a "good report," also in the sentence, "If you have anything to say in his favor, come with him and tell me."[7] In the N.T., when man is said to bless God (Lk. 2:28), the word refers to the act of speaking well of God, of speaking in His favor, of extolling Him for what He is and does, in these senses, of the act of praising Him, of eulogizing Him. The word *aineo* is translated by the word "praise." It means "to extol." *Eulogeo* however, in its intrinsic meaning carries the idea which *aineo* merely refers to. When God is said to bless man (Eph. 1:3), *eulogeo* refers to the act of God in which He elevates man, makes him great, gives him prosperity, confers benefits upon him. When man blesses God, it is an exaltation with words. When God blesses man, it is an exaltation by act, that of conferring benefits upon him. When man is said to bless his fellow man (Lk. 6:28), he confers benefits upon him (Rom. 12:14-21), or speaks well of (Lk. 1:28) in the sense of eulogizing. The word is also used in the sense of asking God's blessing on a thing, praying Him to bless it to one's use, as in Mt. 26:26; I Cor. 10:16. Another use of the word is found in Eph. 1:3 where the noun "blessings" refers to the benefits or favors themselves which are conferred upon man. The verb is found in *Mt.* 5:44, 14:19, 21:9, 23:39, 25:34, 26:26; *Mk.* 6:41, 8:7, 10:16, 11:9, 10, 14:22; *Lk.* 1:28, 42, 64 *(praised),* 2:28, 34, 6:28, 9:16, 13:35, 19:38, 24:30, 50, 51, 53; *John* 12:13; *Acts* 3:26; *Rom.* 12:14; *I Cor.* 4:12, 10:16, 14:16; *Gal.* 3:9; *Eph.* 1:3; *Heb.* 6:14, 7:1, 6, 7, 11:20, 21; *Jas.* 3:9; *I Pet.* 3:9; the

---

6, 7. *Moulton and Milligan, Vocabulary of the Greek Testament.*

adjective in *Mk.* 14:61; *Lk.* 1:68; *Rom.* 1:25, 9:5; *II Cor.* 1:3, 11:31; *Eph.* 1:3; *I Pet.* 1:3; the noun in *Rom.* 15:29, 16:18 (*fair speeches*); *I Cor.* 10:16; *II Cor.* 9:5, 6 (*bounty and bountiful*); *Gal.* 3:14; *Eph.* 1:3; *Heb.* 6:7, 12:17; *Jas.* 3:10; *I Pet.* 3:9; *Rev.* 5:12, 13, 7:12. Make a study of this word in these passages, and see how much light is thrown upon the English translation you are using.

DISCIPLE. From the Greek verb *manthano* which means "to learn, to be apprised of, to increase one's knowledge," there are derived the words *mathetes* which means "a learner, a pupil, one who follows the teaching of someone else," thus, a disciple; and *matheteuo* which means "to follow the precepts and instructions of another," thus to be his disciple; also, "to make a disciple, to teach, to instruct." We must be careful to note that the Greek word for "disciple" does not carry with it the idea that that person who is named a disciple is necessarily a saved person. The word does not contain any implications of salvation. A person may learn something from someone else and yet not put that knowledge into practice or make it a part of his life. See John 6:66 in its context for an example of an unsaved disciple, and Matthew 10:1, for an illustration of saved (the eleven) and unsaved (Judas) discipleship. The word merely refers to one who puts himself under the teaching of someone else and learns from him. For the noun, see your English concordance. The verb is found in Mt. 13:52 (*instructed*), 27:57, 28:19 (*teach*); Acts 14:21 (*taught*). In the case of the word "disciple" the context must rule as to whether the particular disciple mentioned, is saved or unsaved, not the word itself.

DISORDERLY. The verb meaning "to conduct one's self in a disorderly manner" is *atakteo*. It comes from the verb *tasso* which is a military term referring to the act of arranging soldiers in military order in the ranks. When the Greeks wanted to make a word mean the opposite to what it meant originally, they placed the letter Alpha as its first letter. Thus *atakteo* refers to soldiers marching out of order or quitting the ranks, thus being disorderly. The word therefore means "deviating from the prescribed order or rule." Its original meaning was that of riot or rebellion. The word is found only in the Thessalonian epistles, in its verb form in II Thes. 3:7, as an adjective in I Thes. 5:14 (unruly), and as an adverb in II Thes. 3:6, 11.

However, in the Thessalonian epistles, this word is not used in its military sense, but in a metaphorical one. There has been a question as to whether the word referred to actual moral wrongdoing, or to a certain remissness in daily work or routine. The latter meaning is now supported by almost contemporary evidence from the papyri. It appears in a contract dated in A.D. 66, in which a father apprenticed his son to a craftsman. The father enters into an agreement with the craftsman that if there are any days when his son "plays truant" or "fails to attend," he is afterward to make them good. In a manuscript of A.D. 183, a weaver's apprentice must appear for an equivalent number of days, if from idleness or ill-health or any other reason he exceeds the twenty day vacation he is allowed in the year.

The word in II Thessalonians 3:11 most certainly is used in the sense of "playing truant from one's employment," since it is defined by the words, "working not at all," the Greek word *ergazomai* meaning "to labor, do work, to trade, to make gains by trading," which usage is in accord with the meaning of the word at that time. The same is the case with 3:6, 7. Paul supported himself while preaching. The word appears also in I Thessalonians 5:14 (unruly) where it could refer to any deviation from the prescribed order or rule of the Christian life.

PARABLE. This word comes from the Greek *parabole,* which in turn comes from *ballo* "to throw" and *para, "alongside."* Therefore, a parable is an illustration thrown in alongside of a truth to make the latter easier to understand.

SYNAGOGUE. This word comes from *ago* "to go" and *sun* "with." Thus it refers to the act of a group of people "going with one another," thus congregating in one place. Finally, it came to refer to the place where they congregated. The word was used to designate the buildings other than the central Jewish temple where the Jews congregated for worship.

CHURCH. The word *ekklesia* appears in the Greek text where this word is found in the translations. *Ekklesia* comes from *kaleo* "to call," and *ek* "out from." The compound verb means "to call out from." In classical Greek *ekklesia* referred to an assembly of the citizens summoned by the town crier. It is used in Acts 19:32-41 in its purely classical meaning. The town clerk dismissed the citizens who had been gathered together by the craftsmen of Ephesus. In its every other occurrence, it is translated "church," the church being looked upon as a called-out body of people, called out of the world of unsaved humanity to become the people of God. The word refers either to the Mystical Body of Christ made up of saved individuals only (Ephesians), or to the local churches, as for instance Rom. 16:5; Gal. 1:2. The word "assembly" is a good one-word translation of *ekklesia.* The genius of the word points to the fact that in the mind of God, the Church of Jesus Christ is a called-out group of people, separated out from the world to be a people that should maintain their separation from the world out of which they have been called.

REPENT is the translation of *metanoeo* which in classical Greek meant "to change one's mind or purpose, to change one's opinion." The noun *metanoia* meant "a change of mind on reflection." These two words used in classical Greek signified a change of mind regarding anything, but when brought over into the New Testament, their usage is limited to a change of mind in the religious sphere. They refer there to a change of moral thought and reflection which follows moral delinquency. This includes not only the act of changing one's attitude towards and opinion of sin but also that of forsaking it. Sorrow and contrition with respect to sin, are included in the Bible idea of repentance, but these follow and are consequent upon the sinner's change of mind with respect to it. The word *metamelomai* is used in Mt. 21:29, 32, 27:3; II Cor. 7:8; Heb. 7:21, where it is translated "repent." *Metanoeo* is the fuller and nobler term, expressive of moral action and issues. It is the word used by N.T., writers to express the foregoing meaning. In the case of Judas, *metamelomai* means "remorse." In the case of Heb. 7:21 it means only to change one's mind. The act of repentance is based first of all and primarily upon an intellectual apprehension of the character of sin, man's guilt with respect to it, and man's duty to turn away from it. The emotional and volitional aspects of the act of repentance follow, and are the result of this intellectual process of a change of mind with respect to it. This means that the correct approach of the Christian worker to a sinner whom he wishes to lead to the Lord is that of clearly explaining the issues involved. When the unsaved person is made to clearly understand the significance of sin, the intellectual process of changing his mind with respect to it can follow, with the result that sorrow, contrition, and turning away from it will also follow. A mere emotional appeal to the sinner is not the correct one. The Greek word *metanoeo* tells us that the intellectual appeal must come first, since the act of repenting is basically a mental one at the start.

BELIEVE, FAITH, FAITHFULNESS. The verb is *pisteuo*, the noun *pistis*, the adjective *pistos*. In classical Greek *pisteuo* meant *to believe, trust, trust in, put faith in, rely upon* a person or thing. In the passive voice it meant *I am entrusted with a thing, have it committed to me.* *Pistis* meant *trust* in others, *faith*. *Pistos* meant *faithful, trusty, true,* used of persons one believes or trusts.

In the papyri,[8] we find the following illustrations of the use of these words; *Whom no one would trust even if they were willing to work;* (confidence in the person's character and motives) ; *I have trusted no one to take it to her,* (confidence in the ability of another to perform a certain task). *Pisteuo* in every instance is translated by the word "believe," except in the following places; *Lk.* 16:11; *John* 2:24; *Rom.* 3:2; *I Cor.* 9:17; *Gal.* 2:7; *I Thes.* 2:4; *I Tim.* 1:11; *Tit.* 1:3, where the idea is that either of entrusting one's self or something else into the custody and safe keeping of another. *Pistis* is translated in every case except the following by the word *faith;* Acts 17:31 *(assurance)*, and Heb. 10:39, literally *to them who are of faith.* *Pistos* is translated by the words *faithful, believing* and *true.*

When these words refer to the faith which a lost sinner must place in the Lord Jesus in order to be saved, they include the following ideas; the act of considering the Lord Jesus worthy of trust as to His character and motives, the act of placing confidence in His ability to do just what He says He will do, the act of entrusting the salvation of his soul into the hands of the Lord Jesus, the act of committing the work of saving his soul to the care of the Lord. This means a definite taking of one's self out of one's own keeping and entrusting one's self into the keeping of the Lord Jesus.

In *Acts* 8:13, 26:27; *Jas.* 2:19, the word refers merely to an intellectual assent to certain facts, in *Acts* 15:11, to a dogmatic belief that such and such is the case.

---

8. *Moulton and Milligan.*

"The N.T. conception of faith includes three main elements, mutually connected and requisite, though according to circumstances sometimes one and sometimes another may be more prominent, viz., (1) a fully convinced acknowledgement of the revelation of grace; (2) a self-surrendering fellowship (adhesion); and (3) a fully assured and unswerving trust (and with this at the same time hope) in the God of salvation or in Christ. None of these elements is wholly ignored by any of the N.T. writers."[9] Thus, the word sometimes refers to an acknowledgment that a certain statement is true (Mt. 21:25), and sometimes to a definite commitment of one's soul into the keeping of another (John 5:24).

SANCTIFY, SAINT, HOLY, HALLOW. These and their related English words are all translations of the same Greek root. The religious terms of Christianity were taken from those in use in the pagan Greek religions, for the New Testament was written in the international Greek of the Roman world. The Bible writers could not coin new terms since they would not be understood, and were therefore forced to use those already in use. However, while the technical and root meanings of these pagan religious terms were taken over by the writers, yet by their use in the New Testament, their moral and spiritual characters were changed and elevated.

The classical Greek word meaning *to sanctify* is *hagizo* which means to *consecrate,* for instance, altars, sacrifices, *to set apart for the gods, to present, to offer.* The word used in the New Testament answering to *hagizo* is *hagiazo* which means "to place in a relation to God answering to His holiness."[10] Neither word means merely "to set apart," but in the case of the pagan word, "to set apart for the gods," and in the case of the Christian word "to set apart for God." The worshipper of the pagan god acquired the character of that pagan god

9. *Cremer, Biblico-Theological Lexicon of New Testament Greek.*
10. *Cremer.*

and the religious ceremonies connected with its worship. The Greek temple at Corinth housed a large number of harlots who were connected with the worship of the Greek god. Thus, the set-apartness of the Greek worshipper was in character licentious, totally depraved, and sinful. The believer in the Lord Jesus is set apart for God by the Holy Spirit, out of the First Adam with the latter's sin and condemnation, into the Last Adam with the latter's righteousness and life. Thus, the worshipper of the God of the Bible partakes of the character of the God for whom he is set apart. This is positional sanctification, an act of God performed at the moment a sinner puts his faith in the Lord Jesus (I Cor. 1:2). The work of the Holy Spirit in the yielded saint, in which He sets the believer apart for God in his experience, by eliminating sin from his life and producing His fruit, a process which goes on constantly throughout the believer's life, is called progressive sanctification (I Thes. 5:23). When our Lord sanctifies Himself, He sets Himself apart for God as the Sacrifice for sin (John 17:19; Heb. 10:7). When man sanctifies God, "the word denotes that manner of treatment on the part of man which corresponds with the holiness of God, and which springs from faith, trust, and fear" (I Pet. 3:15).[11] In the case where the unbelieving wife is sanctified by the believing husband, and the unbelieving husband is sanctified by the believing wife, it "clearly cannot signify the sanctification in its fulness which the N.T. divine and saving work produces; for a personal faith is required in the object of it, which is in this case denied. Still it is unmistakably intimated that by virtue of the marriage union, the unbelieving side in its measure participates in the saving work and fellowship with God experienced by the believing side."[12]

The word *saint* is the translation of *hagios*. This word is one of the five words the Greeks used to express the idea of holiness, insofar as they had any conception of that quality.

11, 12. *Cremer.*

It is the one used most rarely. It is the only Greek word used in the Bible to express the idea of the biblical conception of holiness. The biblical content of the word is not found in any or all of the five Greek words for holiness, except the ideas of "the consecrated, the sublime, the venerable." The main elements such as morality, spirituality, purity, are entirely wanting. Thus this pagan Greek word had to be filled with an additional content of meaning and in that sense coined afresh.

Hagios appears to have been specially used of temples or places of worship, of those places consecrated to the gods which claimed general reverence. *Hagios* was used to designate that which deserved and claimed moral and religious reverence.

As to the biblical use of *hagios* as expressing the idea of God's holiness, Cremer says, "God's holiness signifies His opposition to sin manifesting itself in atonement and redemption or in judgment. . . . Holiness is the perfect purity of God which in and for itself excludes all fellowship with the world, and can only establish a relationship of free electing love, whereby it asserts itself in the sanctification of God's people, their cleansing and redemption; there the purity of God manifesting itself in atonement and redemption, and correspondingly in judgment." The word is used "of men and things occupying the relation to God which is conditioned and brought about by His holiness, whether it be that God has chosen them for His service, as instruments of His work, or that God's holiness has sanctified them and taken them into the fellowship of the redeeming God, the God of salvation."[13]

This word *hagios* is used as a name for the Christian believer (Rom. 1:7). As such it refers to him as one set apart for God, partaking of a holy standing before God in Christ Jesus (I Cor. 1:30 *sanctification*), with the obligation of living a holy life (I Pet. 1:15, 16).

---

13. *Cremer.*

FELLOWSHIP, COMMUNION. These two words are the translation of *koinonia*. This Greek word is used in a marriage contract where the husband and wife agree to a *joint-participation* in the necessaries of life. The key idea in the word is that of a partnership, a possessing things in common, a belonging in common to. For instance, "What things does light have in common with darkness?" (II Cor. 6:14), or, "These things write we unto you that ye also may have joint-participation with us" (in our knowledge of the life of our Lord) (I John 1:3), or, "Our joint-participation is with the Father and with His Son Jesus Christ" (I John 1:3), that is, the things in which Christians participate in salvation, they participate in jointly with God, a common nature, common likes and dislikes; or, "The cup of blessing which we bless, is it not a joint-participation (which we saints have in common) in the blood of Christ? The bread which we break, is it not a joint-participation (which we saints have in common) in the body of Christ" (broken for us) (I Cor. 10:16)? That is, the saints participate in common with one another in the salvation benefits that proceed from the out-poured blood and the broken body of the Lord Jesus. In the light of the usage of the word *koinonia,* make a study of the following places where the word occurs, *I Cor.* 1:9; *II Cor.* 6:14, 8:4, 13:14; *Gal.* 2:9; *Eph.* 3:9; *Phil.* 1:5, 2:1, 3:10; *I John* 1:3, 6, 7. In *Acts* 2:42 and *I John* 1:3, 6, 7, the usage of the word also approaches the common usage of today, that of fellowship in the sense of companionship. In *Phil.* 2:1 and *II Cor.* 13:14 the word refers to the joint-participation of the believer and the Holy Spirit in a common interest and activity in the things of God. Study the usage of the word in *Rom.* 15:26 (contribution); *II Cor.* 9:13 (distribution); *Phm.* 6 (communication); *Heb.* 13:16 (to communicate).

PREDESTINATE is the translation of *proorizo* which is made up of *horizo* "to divide or separate from as a border or boundary, to mark out boundaries, to mark out, to determine, appoint," and *pro* "before." Thus, the compound word means "to divide or separate from a border or boundary beforehand, to determine or appoint beforehand." The genius of the word is that of placing limitations upon someone or something beforehand, these limitations bringing that person or thing within the sphere of a certain future or destiny. These meanings are carried over into the New Testament usage of the word. Thus, the "chosen-out" ones, have had limitations put around them which bring them within the sphere of becoming God's children by adoption (Eph. 1:5), and of being conformed to the image of the Lord Jesus (Rom. 8:29). See the other occurrences of *proorizo* in Acts 4:28; I Cor. 2:7; Eph. 1:11.

CHOOSE is from *eklegomai* which is made up of *lego* "to choose" and *ek* "out from." Thus, the compound word means "to pick, single out, to choose out." The genius of the word has in it the idea of not merely choosing, but that of choosing out from a number. The adjective *eklektos* comes from *eklegomai* and is translated by the words "chosen" and "elect." The elect are "the chosen-out ones." Divine election refers therefore to the act of God in which He chooses out certain from among mankind for salvation. This election does not imply the rejection of the rest, but is the outcome of the love of God lavished upon those chosen-out. Cremer says that "it is unwarranted to give special prominence either to the element of *selection from among others,* or to that of *preference above others.* The main import is that of *appointment for a certain object or goal.*" See John 15:16, 19; Eph. 1:4.

FOREKNOWLEDGE is the translation of *prognosis* (the noun) (Acts 2:23; I Pet. 1:2). *Proginosko,* the verb, is translated *foreknow* (Rom. 8:29), *foreknew* (Rom. 11:2), and *foreordained* (I Pet. 1:20). *Proginosko* in classical Greek

meant "to know, perceive, learn, or understand beforehand."
It implied a previous knowledge of a thing. It is used in its
purely classical sense in Acts 26:5 and II Peter 3:17. But both
prognosis and *proginosko* in other places in the New Testament have by their use in relationship to God, acquired an
additional content of meaning.

The first occurrence of either one, the usage of which determines the usage of both in other places in the New Testament is in Acts 2:23, where *prognosis* is used. These words,
when used of God in the New Testament, signify more than
merely the fact of knowing something beforehand. That is a
self-evident attribute of the omniscient God. The Bible wastes
no space on self-evident facts. The words *determinate counsel
and foreknowledge of God* (Acts 2:23), are in a construction
in Greek which shows that the word *foreknowledge* refers to
the same act that the words *determinate counsel* refer to, and
is a farther description of that act. The word *counsel* refers
to the results of a consultation between individuals, the word
determinate describing this consultation as one that had for
its purpose the fixing of limits upon, thus determining the
destiny of someone, here, that of the Lord Jesus. In the councils of the Trinity, it was decided that the Lord Jesus should
be given over into the hands of wicked men. The word
prognosis refers to the same act, and therefore includes in it
the idea in the words *determinate counsel*. It adds, however
the idea of the foreordination of the Person whose destiny
was decided upon in the council referred to. This word did
not have this meaning in classical Greek. It was inevitable
that when words of a pagan people were brought over into the
New Testament, they often acquired an additional content of
meaning by reason of the advanced conceptions of Christianity and its supernatural character. The translators of the
Authorized Version used the word *foreordained* in I Pet. 1:20.
The translation should be *foreordination* in Acts 2:23 and I
Pet. 1:2, and *foreordained* in Rom. 8:29, 11:2.

JUSTIFY. The words *justify, justification, righteous, righteousness, just, right, meet,* are all translations of the same Greek root. The verb *justify* is *dikaioo,* the noun *righteousness, dikaiosune,* the adjective *righteous, dikaios.* This means that all these words have a general meaning that is common to all of them, even though their individual meaning may differ slightly. This again means that there is a definite and vital connection between the act of justifying and the righteousness of the individual who has been justified. We will look first at the usage of these words in pagan Greek literature. "In pagan Greece the *dikaios* person is he who does not selfishly nor yet self-for-gettingly transgress the bounds fixed for him, and gives to everyone his own, yet still desires what is his, and does not in the least withdraw the assertion of his own claims."[14] Paul uses *dikaios* in its purely classical sense in Rom. 5:7. In the biblical sense, *dikaios* is "what is right, conformable to right, answering to the claims of usage, custom, or right. ... The fundamental idea is that of a state or condition conformable to order, apart from the consideration whether usage or custom or other factors determine the order or direction. Thus, *dikaios* is synonymous with *agathos* (good), only that *dikaios* is a conception of a relation and presupposes a norm, whereas the subject of *agathos* is its own norm."[15]

In understanding the words *justify* and *righteous,* as they are used in the New Testament, it should always be kept in mind that their meaning is not a *subjective* one but an *objective* one. That is, the content of meaning in these words is not to be determined by each individual Bible expositor. If that were the case, what is righteous one day, may not be righteous the next. The content of meaning in that case would be dependent upon the fluctuating standards and ethics of men. With the present trend towards the teaching of the relativity of all truth, this method of interpretation be-

---

14. *Cremer.*
15, 16. *Cremer.*

comes a most vicious thing. What is right one day may be wrong the next.

God is the objective standard which determines the content of meaning of *dikaios*, and at the same time keeps that content of meaning constant and unchanging, since He is the unchanging One. "Righteousness in the biblical sense is a condition of rightness the standard of which is God, which is estimated according to the divine standard, which shows itself in behavior conformable to God, and has to do above all things with its relation to God, and with the walk before Him. It is, and it is called *dikaiosune theou* (righteousness of God) (Rom. 3:21, 1:17), righteousness as it belongs to God, and is of value before Him, Godlike righteousness, see Eph. 4:24; with this righteousness thus defined, the gospel (Rom. 1:17) comes into the world of nations which had been wont to measure by a different standard. Righteousness in the Scripture sense is a thoroughly religious conception, designating the normal relation of men and their acts, etc., to God. Righteousness in the profane mind is a preponderatingly social virtue, only with a certain religious background."[16]

Justification in the Bible sense therefore is the act of God removing from the believing sinner, his guilt and the penalty incurred by that guilt, and bestowing a positive righteousness, Christ Jesus Himself in whom the believer stands, not only innocent and uncondemned, but actually righteous in point of law for time and for eternity. The words *justify, justification, righteous, righteousness*, as used of man in his relation to God, have a legal, judicial basis. God is the Judge, man the defendant. God is the standard of all righteousness. The white linen curtains of the court of the Tabernacle, symbolized the righteousness which God is, the righteousness which God demands of any human being who desires to fellowship with Him, and the righteousness which God provides on the basis of the acceptance on the sinner's part, of the Lord Jesus who

perfectly satisfied the just demands of God's holy law which
we broke. A just person therefore is one who has been thus
declared righteous (Rom. 1:17). The word is used in its non-
legal sense in Phil. 1:7 and Lk. 12:57 for instance, where it
speaks of conduct that is conformable to what is right.

PROPITIATION. In Rom. 3:25; I John 2:2, 4:10, our
Lord is said to be the propitiation with reference to our sins.
The word in Rom. 3:25 is *hilasterion,* and in I John 2:2, 4:10,
hilasmos. These words were used in the Greek pagan religions, *hilasterion,* "an expiatory sacrifice," *hilasmos,* "a means
of appeasing." The word *appeasing* strikes the keynote meaning of both words. The pagan offered a sacrifice as a means
of appeasing the anger and displeasure of his god. Pope has
a couplet, "Let fierce Achilles, dreadful in his rage. The god
propitiate, and the pest assuage." The word *propitiate* here
means "to appease and render favorable, to conciliate." That
was the pagan usage of *hilasterion* and *hilasmos.* But the
petty peevishness, irascibility, and petulant anger of a pagan
deity is not to be brought over into the New Testament meaning of these words. The attitude of the God of the Bible
towards sinners is not comparable to that of the imagined
attitude of a pagan god towards his worshippers.

In its biblical usage, *hilasmos* means "an expiation." Our
Lord is the *hilasmos* in that He became the Sacrifice on the
Cross which perfectly met the demands of the broken law.
The word is used in the LXX in Levit. 25:9 and Num. 5:8,
and is in both cases translated by the word *atonement.* The
word "expiation" means "to extinguish the guilt of by suffer-
ance of penalty or some equivalent, to make satisfaction for,
to atone for." The word *hilasterion* is used in the LXX in
Levit. 16:14, of the golden cover of the Ark of the Covenant
upon which was sprinkled the atoning blood. It is translated
mercy seat in Heb. 9:5. *Hilasmos* is "that which propitiates,"
and *hilasterion* is "the place of propitiation." Our Lord is
both. *In the biblical usage of these words, the thought is not*

that of placating the anger of a vengeful God, but that of satisfying the righteous demands of His justice so that His government might be maintained, and that mercy might be shown on the basis of justice duly satisfied.

The verb *hilaskomai*, which has the same root as *hilasterion* and *hilasmos*, is used in Lk. 18:13 and Heb. 2:17. The word in classical Greek meant "to appease, to sooth, to make propitious to one, to reconcile one's self to another." In Homer, it was always used of gods, to make the gods propitious, to cause them to be reconciled, to worship them. The pagan usage of *hilaskomai* is in the last analysis a procedure by which something is to be made good. It is used, for instance, where someone had wronged a person and after the latter's death, had paid him divine honors as somehow making things right, appeasing the outraged feelings of the dead man. The act of appeasing a god indicates that goodwill was not conceived to be the original and natural condition of the gods, but something that must first be earned. The word was used where someone wished to gain the goodwill of Apollo so that he would feel inclined to deliver an oracle.

When *hilaskomai* is used in the New Testament, Cremer says that God is never the object of the action denoted in the verb. It never means "to conciliate God." The heathen, he says, believed the deity to be naturally alienated in feeling from man; and though the energetic manifestation of this feeling is specially excited by sin, man has to suffer for it. Thus, the purpose of the propitiatory sacrifices and prayers that were offered, was to effect a change in this feeling. The occasion for this offering could be after the person had sinned, or it could be at a time when there was no distinct consciousness of particular guilt, but simply for the purpose of securing the favor of the god. But in the Bible, the situation is different. God is not of Himself already alienated from man. God is as to His nature, love, and He loves the sinner. Witness the statement in John 3:16. His feelings with respect to the

human race need not be changed. But the sin of man placed
an obstacle in God's way when He in His infinite love desired
to bless man with salvation, and that obstacle was the broken
law and the guilt of man. The former cried out for justice
to be satisfied, and the latter needed to be cleansed away.
Thus, in order that it would not be necessary for Him to
demand that the penalty be meted out upon guilty mankind
so that He might satisfy the demands of His broken law, and
in order that He might lavish His mercy upon man on the
basis of justice satisfied, He Himself became the expiation
demanded by His holiness and justice. There is no thought
here of God placating Himself, or of rendering Himself
conciliatory to Himself, or of appeasing His own anger. The
thought would be ridiculous. It is a purely legal operation.
The Judge takes upon Himself the penalty of the one whom
He has adjudged guilty, and thus can show mercy. The
judgment seat becomes a mercy seat. When the publican
asked God to be merciful to him the sinner (Lk. 18:13), he
really asked Him to offer that sacrifice for his sin which
would put that sin away and thus allow a holy and a righteous God to bless him with salvation. The verb *hilaskomai*
appears in the text. He was looking ahead to the accomplish-
ment of the work of salvation at the Cross. His faith stretched
out to that event and laid hold of it. It is neither scriptural
nor is it good practice to ask a seeking sinner today to pray
that prayer, either in the sense of the meaning of *hilaskomai*
or in the sense of asking God to be merciful to him. He
should be taught that God has paid the penalty for his sin,
and God's mercy on that basis is extended to him, and that
on the basis of what God has done at the Cross, he should by
faith appropriate the salvation God offers him. The verb
hilaskomai is found in Heb. 2:17, where it is translated "to
make reconciliation for." We have noted all the places where
these three words occur in the New Testament.

CONFESS. This word is the translation of *homologeo* which is rendered uniformly throughout the New Testament by the word *confess* except in the following places; *Mt.* 7:23 (*profess*), 14:7 (*promised*); *I Tim.* 6:12; *Tit.* 1:16 (*profess*); *Heb.* 13:15 (*giving thanks*). The related noun *homologia* is translated in *II Cor.* 9:13, *I Tim.* 6:12, 13, *Heb.* 3:1, 4:14, 10:23, either by *profession* or *confession*. *Homologeo* is made up of the words *homos* (*same*), and *lego* (*to speak*). Thus, the word means "to say the same thing" as another, hence, "to agree with, to assent to a thing." It had various uses in classical Greek; "to speak or say together, to speak one language, to agree with, to make an agreement, to come to terms, the latter meaning used especially of persons surrendering in war, to agree to a thing, to allow, admit, confess, grant," the latter found in the sentence *I grant you;* the noun means "an agreement, a compact; in war, terms of surrender; an assent, an admission, a confession."

The papyri give examples of the Koine use of the word. There is an agreement between two individuals, a person gives his consent, another one acknowledges having found something. The noun is used of a contract, an agreement.

With these usages in mind, we will study a few representative places where the word is found. In I John 1:9, confession of sin on the part of the Christian is not a mere admission of the same to God. The act of confession includes the act of the Christian in coming to terms with God in regard to his sin, of agreeing with God as to what He says about that sin and what the Christian ought to do about it, the entering into a contract or agreement with Him that if He will cleanse that Christian from the defilement of that sin, the latter will not be repeated. In Lk. 12:8, confession of Christ means the public acknowledgment of Him and all that He is and stands for. The act of confession implies that the one confessing the Lord Jesus, has come to agree with the Bible's estimate of Him. In I John 4:2, the word refers to a public acknowledgment of the fact that one has come to the place where he is in agreement with the facts revealed in Scripture concerning Jesus Christ. In Mt. 7:23, it means "to say openly, not to keep silence," in Mt. 14:7, "to concede, to engage, to promise." In the latter case, Herod entered into contract with the daughter of Herodias to give her whatever she asked.

In the word, there is the idea of a person agreeing with someone or something, of entering into a contract with someone, of assenting to the statement of another, of coming to terms with another. When interpreting the word in its occurrences in the New Testament, search for the particular shade of meaning demanded by the context.

GOSPEL. In every case, this word is the translation of *euaggelion*. The verb is *euaggelizomai*. The word *eu* meant in classical Greek, "well" in its kind, as opposed to the Greek word *kakos* which meant "bad, evil, bad" in its kind, "ugly, hideous," and *aggello* which meant "to bear a message, bring tidings or news, proclaim." Thus, the verb means "to bring a message of good news," and the noun, "good news." The word "gospel" comes from the Saxon word *gode-spell*, the word *gode* meaning *good*, and "spell" meaning *a story, a tale*. The word *euaggelion* was in just as common use in the first century as our words *good news*. "Have you any good news (*euaggelion*) for me today?" must have been a common question. Our word *gospel* today has a definite religious connotation. In the ordinary conversation of the first century, it did not have such a meaning. However, it was taken over into the Cult of the Caesar where it acquired a religious significance. The Cult of the Caesar was the state religion of the Roman empire, in which the emperor was worshipped as a god. When the announcement of the emperor's birthday was made, or the accession of a new Caesar proclaimed, the account of either event was designated by the word *euaggelion*.

Thus, when the Bible writers were announcing the good news of salvation, they used the word *euaggelion*, which word meant to the first century readers "good news." See how this helps one in the understanding of a verse like Heb. 4:2, "for unto us (first-century Jews) was the good news (of salvation in Christ) preached, as well as the good news (of a land flowing with milk and honey) to them (the generation which came out of Egypt)." There is the good news of the kingdom (Mt. 4:23) announced at the First Advent and rejected, to be announced at the Second Advent and accepted by Israel, good news to the effect that the Lord Jesus is the High Priest who saves the believer, and also King of kings who will reign as the world Sovereign. There is the good news of Jesus Christ (I Cor. 9:12), which is good news concerning Jesus Christ, namely, that He died on the Cross and thus becomes the Saviour of the sinner who puts his faith in Him. There is the good news of the grace of God (Acts 20:24), referring to the same thing as the good news of Jesus Christ.

The verb *euaggelizomai* is uniformly translated "to preach the gospel" except where it may be rendered "bring or show glad (good) tidings," or "hath declared." In the following places it is translated by the word "preach," but since there is a Greek word that means "to preach" in the sense of "to announce," *kerusso*, the translation should be expanded to include the idea of good news: *Lk.* 3:18, 4:43, 16:16; *Acts* 5:42, 8:4, 12, 35, 40, 10:36, 11:20, 14:7, 15:35, 17:18; I Cor. 15:1, 2; *Gal.* 1:16, 23; *Eph.* 2:17, 3:8; *Heb.* 4:6; *Rev.* 14:6. Thus, one should translate for instance, "The kingdom of God is preached as glad tidings," or, "preaching the Word as good news," or, "preaching the Lord Jesus as good tidings."

The word *evangelist* comes from the Greek *euaggelistes*, a bringer of good tidings.

BOWELS. This word is the translation of *splagchnon* which in classical Greek referred to the inward parts, especially to the nobler parts of the inner organs, the heart, lungs, and liver. It was the oriental metaphor for our "heart," the seat of the feelings, affections. In the Greek poets, the bowels were regarded as the seat of the more violent passions such as anger and love, but by the Hebrews as the seat of the tenderer affections, kindness, benevolence and compassion. In a manuscript of B.C. 5, it was used in the phrase "for pity's sake."[17] In its metaphorical usage in the New Testament, it means what we in the occident speak of as the heart. It refers to the emotions of compassion, pity, the tenderer affections. As in classical Greek, it is also used to refer to the literal parts of the body. The only place in the N.T., where it is so used is in Acts 1:18. In Lk. 1:78, the words *tender mercy* are in the Greek *splagchna,* the word for *bowels.* Thus, the idea in the word is that of the tender affections. In II Cor. 7:15, the word is translated *inward affection.* In other places, it is translated by the word *bowels.* It would be better to have translated II Cor. 6:12, "Ye are compressed (cramped) in your own affections." Paul had just told them, "Ye are not straitened (compressed or cramped) in us;" that is, "ample space is granted you in our heart." Then he says, "Ye are straitened (compressed or cramped) in your own affections, so that there is no room there for us;" that is, "you do not grant a place in your heart for love to me." Paul in Phil. 1:8 longs after the Philippians with the tender-heartednesses of Jesus Christ. In Phil. 2:1 he speaks of tender-heartednesses and mercies. In Col. 3:12, he exhorts the saints to have a heart of mercy and kindness. In Phm. 7, Philemon's beautiful Christian life refreshes the affectionate natures of the saints. Paul sends the runaway slave Onesimus back to his master, and says, "whom I have sent again, him, that is, my own bowels" (v. 12). The great apostle who had led Onesimus to the Lord, had so come to love him, that when he sent him back to Philemon, his heart went with him. The word *receive* is not in the best texts. He exhorts Philemon to refresh his heart, his tender emotions (v. 20). In I John 3:17 *splagchnon* is translated

---

17. *Moulton and Milligan.*

"bowels of compassion." The idea is, the shutting up of one's compassionate heart.

In the Gospel statements concerning our Lord, such as "He was moved with compassion," the word is *splagchnizomai,* the same word translated "bowels," but in the verb form. The word in its root therefore refers to a heart of compassion, kindness, pity, mercy, to the tenderer affections as produced in the heart of the yielded believer by the Holy Spirit.

BEAST. There are two Greek words translated by the one word "beast" in the Book of The Revelation. These Greek words have different meanings. For a proper appreciation of the places where they are found, the English reader should know the distinctive meaning of each word, and where each word is found.

The word *zoon* in classical Greek meant "a living being, an animal." The Greek word for "life" is *zoe.* The word *zoon* therefore refers to a living organism, whether animal or human, the emphasis being upon the fact that it is alive as opposed to the state of death. It is found in the following places in The Revelation, 4:6, 7, 8, 9, 5:6, 8, 11, 14, 6:1, 3, 5, 6, 7, 7:11, 14:3, 15:7, 19:4. In each case, the translation should read "living creature." These living creatures are the Cherubim. They are first mentioned in Gen. 3:24. They were the guardians of the entrance to Eden. Golden figures of these cherubim were carved out of one piece of gold with the Mercy Seat (Ex. 25:10-22). Ezekiel speaks of cherubim in Ezek. 1. The other places where *zoon* is used are Heb. 13:11; II Pet. 2:12; Jude 10.

The other word is *therion,* which in classical Greek referred to a wild animal, a wild beast, a savage beast that is hunted, a poisonous animal, a reptile. This word is found in The Revelation in 6:8, 11:7, 13:1, 2, 3, 4, 11, 12, 14, 15, 17, 18, 14:9, 11, 15:2, 16:2, 10, 13, 17:3, 7, 8, 11, 12, 13, 16, 17, 19:19, 20, 20:4, 10. In every place except 6:8 where literal wild beasts are referred to, and 13:11, where the false prophet is mentioned, the word "beast" (*therion*) refers to the Antichrist, future head of the revived Roman empire. He is the wild Beast. The other places where *therion* is used are *Mk.* 1:13; *Acts* 10:12, 11:6; 28:4, 5; *Tit.* 1:12; *Heb.* 12:20; *Jas.* 3:7.

TEMPLE. There are two Greek words which are both translated by the one word "temple" in the A.V. Each has its distinctive meaning and refers to a particular thing. It is obvious that if the English reader expects to arrive at a full-orbed interpretation of the passages where the word "temple" is used, he must know which word is used in the Greek text, and the meaning of that distinctive word.

The first word we will study is *hieron*. It is taken from classical Greek, coming from the adjective *hieros*. The latter meant "belonging to or connected with the gods." It meant "holy, hallowed, consecrated," and was used of earthly things devoted or dedicated by man to a god or to the service of a god. It was used sometimes in opposition to several Greek words which meant "profane," that is, "secular," as opposed to "sacred." Thus the building set apart and dedicated to the worship and service of the god was called a *hieron*. This word was taken over into the N.T., and used to designate the temple at Jerusalem. It is the all-inclusive word signifying the whole compass of the sacred enclosure, with its porticos, courts, and other subordinate buildings.

The other word is *naos*, which referred to the temple itself, composed of the Holy of Holies and the Holy Place.

When our Lord taught in the temple, He taught in the *hieron*, in one of the temple porches. He expelled the moneychangers from the *hieron*, the court of the Gentiles. When the veil of the temple was rent at the time of the death of our Lord, it was the veil of the *naos*, the curtain separating the Holy of Holies from the Holy Place. When Zacharias entered the temple to burn incense, he entered the *naos*, the Holy

Place where the altar of incense stood. The people were "without," in the *hieron*. Our Lord spoke of the temple (*naos*) of His body. Paul speaks of the body of the Christian as the temple (*naos*), the inner sanctuary of the Holy Spirit.

The word "temple" is a good translation of *hieron*, the words "inner sanctuary," of *naos*.

Hieron is found in the following places: *Mt.* 4:5, 12:5, 6, 21:12, 14, 15, 23, 24:1, 26:55; *Mk.* 11:11, 15, 16, 27, 12:35, 13:1, 3, 14:49; *Lk.* 2:27, 37, 46, 4:9, 18:10, 19:45, 47, 20:1, 21:5, 37, 38, 22:52, 53, 24:53; John 2:14, 15, 5:14, 7:14, 28, 8:2, 20, 59, 10:23, 11:56, 18:20; *Acts* 2:46, 3:1, 2, 3, 8, 10, 4:1, 5:20, 21, 24, 25, 42, 19:27, 21:26, 27, 28, 29, 30, 22:17, 24:6, 12, 18, 25: 8, 26:21, *I Cor.* 9:13.

Naos is found in the following places: *Mt.* 23:16, 17, 21, 35, 26:61, 27:5, 40, 51; *Mk.* 14:58, 15:29, 38; *Lk.* 1:9, 21, 22, 23:45; John 2:19, 20, 21; *Acts* 7:48, 17:24, 19:24; *I Cor.* 3:16, 17, 6:19; *II Cor.* 6:16; *Eph.* 2:21; *II Thes.* 2:4; *Rev.* 3:12, 7:15, 11:1, 2, 19, 14:15, 17, 15:5, 6, 8, 16:1, 17, 21:22.

Make a study of each place where the word "temple" is found in the N.T., interpreting the passage in the light of the distinctive meaning of the particular Greek word, and see what a flood of additional light is thrown upon the English translation and the passage in question.

FORSAKEN. This word is the translation of *egkataleipo*, which latter is made up of three words, *eg* meaning *in*, *kata* meaning *down*, and *leipo* meaning *to leave*. The composite word means literally *to leave down in*, and was used of a person who let another person down in a set of circumstances that were against him. The word has various meanings: "to abandon, desert, leave in straits, leave helpless, leave destitute, leave in the lurch, let one down." Study Mt. 27:46; Mk. 15:34, and Psalm 22:1 (same Greek word used in LXX), and apply these various meanings. See Acts 2:27 where the words *wilt leave* are from *egkataleipo*, and the word *hell* is the translation of *haides* which is brought over into English in the names Hades, which latter refers here to the place of the departed righteous dead called Abraham's bosom (Lk. 16:22) or paradise (Lk. 23:43). Study the use of the word in II Cor. 4:9. See what light the use of the word throws upon Demas in II Tim. 4:10, as to his status with respect to salvation, as to his relationship to the apostle Paul, as to his responsibility at the time when Paul was in prison. Visualize Paul's aloneness at his trial before the Roman emperor, in the use of *egkataleipo* in II Tim. 4:16. Relate the use of the word in Mt. 27:46 with that in Heb. 13:5. Choose the particular meaning of the word in Heb. 10:25. The word has a special use in Rom. 9:29 where it means "leave surviving."

HELL. There are three Greek words, each referring to a different place, all of which are translated by the one word *hell*, a fact that causes considerable confusion in interpreting the passages where they occur. These words are *geenna, haides*, and *tartaroo*. The first comes into English in the word *Gehenna*, the second, in the word *Hades*, and the third, in the word *Tartarus*.

Geenna refers to the final abode of the wicked dead, called The Lake of Fire in The Revelation (20:14, 15). Where this word occurs, the translation should be *hell*. It is found in *Mt*. 5:22, 29, 30, 10:28, 18:9, 23:15, 33; *Mk*. 9:43, 45, 47; *Lk*. 12:5; *Jas*. 3:6.

Haides refers to the temporary abode of the dead before the resurrection and ascension of the Lord Jesus, the part reserved for the wicked dead, called *haides* (Lk. 16:23), the other for the righteous dead, called Abraham's bosom (Lk. 16:22), paradise (Lk. 23:43),[18] *haides* (Acts 2:27, 31); and to the temporary abode of the wicked dead from those events until the Great White Throne judgment, the righteous dead going at once to be with the Lord (Phil. 1:23; II Cor. 5:8).

---

18. *But not II Cor.* 12:4, *which is heaven.*

The word *haides* is from the Greek stem *id* which means "to see," and the Greek letter Alpha prefixed which makes the composite word mean "not to see," the noun meaning "the unseen." The word itself in its noun form refers to the unseen world made up of all moral intelligences not possessing a physical body. These would include the holy angels, the fallen angels, the demons, the wicked dead, and the righteous dead. As to the inhabitants in the unseen world, the holy angels are in heaven, the fallen angels in Tartarus, the wicked dead in Hades, the righteous dead in heaven, and the demons in the atmosphere of the earth and in the bottomless pit. All these are included in the unseen world. The context should decide as to whether the Greek word *haides* should be transliterated or translated. Where the context deals with departed human beings and their place of abode in the unseen world, it would seem that the word should be transliterated, and the specific name "Hades" be given that place. These places are *Mt.* 11:23; *Lk.* 10:15, 16:23; *Acts* 2:27, 31; *Rev.* 6:8, 20:13, 14. Where the context refers to the unseen world as a whole, the word should be translated, as for instance: Mt. 16:18, "the gates (councils) of the Unseen," namely, the councils of Satan in the unseen world, shall not prevail against the church; or Rev. 1:18, "I have the keys of the Unseen and of death." Our Lord controls the entire unseen world.

Tartarosas is the word in II Pet. 2:4 "cast down to hell." The fallen angels were sent to their temporary prison house, *Tartarus*, until the Great White Throne judgment. Make a study of these places where the word "hell" occurs, in the light of the distinctive Greek word found in each place, and see how much better you understand these passages.

FORM. When this word is used as a noun in the N.T., the Greek word *morphe* appears in the text. *Morphe* is a Greek philosophical term which refers to the outward expression one gives of himself, that outward expression proceeding from and being truly representative of one's inward character and nature. We use the word "form" in that way in the sentence, "The tennis-player's form was excellent." We mean that the outward expression he gave of his inward ability to play tennis, was excellent. The verb is *morphoomai,* which word refers to the act of a person giving outward expression of his true inward character, that outward expression proceeding from and truly representing his true inward nature. *Morphe* is used in Phil. 2:6, 7 in the expressions, "Who being in the form of God," and "took upon Him the form of a servant." The first refers to our Lord being in that state of being in which He gives outward expression of His inner intrinsic essence, that of deity, that outward expression proceeding from and truly representing His essential nature, that of deity. The second refers to Him in the period of His humiliation when He gave outward expression of His inmost nature, that of a bondservant serving others in all humility, that outward expression proceeding from and being truly representative of His inmost nature. Both outward expressions came from His inmost nature as God. The one had to be temporarily laid aside in order that the other could be manifested. The other place where *morphe* is found is in Mk. 16:12 where it is said that Jesus "appeared in another form." This was the occurrence on the road to Emmaus. The word "another" is from *heteros* meaning "another of a different kind." That is, our Lord's outward expression of Himself at that time was of a nature different from the one by which these disciples would have ordinarily known Him, this outward expression proceeding from and being truly representative of His inner nature. It was the glorified Christ clothed with the enswathement of glory that is native to His glorified body.

The verb *morphoomai* is used in Gal. 4:19 in the phrase "until Christ be formed in you." Using our definition of *morphe,* we could translate, "Until Christ be outwardly expressed in you, that outward expression proceeding from and being truly representative of Him." These Galatian saints had ceased to depend upon the Holy Spirit to express the Lord Jesus in their lives, and were depending upon self-effort to obey the Mosaic law. Thus, Christ Jesus was not being outwardly expressed in their lives.

The word *morphosis,* having the same root as *morphe,* is found in Rom. 2:20, and II Tim. 3:5. In the former passage, the religious but unsaved Jew has the form of knowledge and of the truth, in that the outward expression of both in his life and teaching is the mere outward expression of an intellectual but not a heart grasp of the same. Thus we would speak of it as a mere form, an empty pretense lacking reality so far as the saving work of God is concerned. In II Tim. 3:5, these having a form of godliness, exhibit in their lives an outward expression of godliness which proceeds from and is truly representative of an inner state of godliness, but a godliness that is not the genuine godliness associated with salvation, but an imitation one that denies the power of God to save.

TRANSFIGURED. This word occurs in Mt. 17:2; Mk. 9:2. The Greek word is *metamorphoomai.* The word *meta,* prefixed to *morphoomai* signifies a change. The sentence, "He was transfigured before them," in an expanded translation could read: "His outward expression was changed before them, which outward expression proceeded from and was truly representative of His inward being." Our Lord's usual expression of Himself during the days of His earthly life was that of the Man Christ Jesus, a Man of sorrows and acquainted with grief, the Servant come to serve (Phil. 2:7). Now, He gives outward expression of the glory of the essence of His deity, that glory shining right through His human body and nature, that expression proceeding from and being truly representative of His intrinsic deity which He possessed. As a result, His face shone as the sun, and His raiment was white as the light.

TRANSFORM. In Rom. 12:2 this word is the translation of *metamorphoomai,* the same word translated "transfigured" in Mt. 17:2 and Mk. 9:2. The exhortation to the saints is to change their outward expression which they had before they were saved, which outward expression proceeded from and was truly representative of their totally depraved natures, to an outward expression which proceeds from and is truly representative of their new divine natures.

The word "transform" is used also in II Cor. 11:13-15. But here it is the translation of a word that has the opposite meaning to *metamorphoomai.* The word is *metaschematizo* which means "to change one's outward expression by assuming from the outside an expression that does not proceed from nor is it representative of one's true inner nature." The word "masquerade" is an exact English translation. Satan was originally the holy angel Lucifer. As such he gave outward expression of his inner nature as an angel of light, which expression proceeded from and was truly representative of that nature. That was *morphoomai.* Then he sinned and became an angel of darkness, giving outward expression of that darkness. That was *morphoomai.* Then he changed his outward expression from that of darkness to one of light by assuming from the outside, an expression of light, which outward expression did not come from nor was it representative of his inner nature as an angel of darkness. That is *metaschematizo.* The translation could read: "masquerading as the apostles of Christ;" "Satan masquerades as an angel of light;" "his ministers masquerade as the ministers of righteousness."

CONFORM. This word in Rom. 12:2 is the translation of *sunschematizo* which means "to assume an outward expression that is patterned after something else, which outward expression does not come from within and is not representative of one's inward nature, but which is assumed from without." Paul is exhorting the saints not to assume an outward expression which is patterned after the world, which is assumed from without, and which does not come from nor is it representative of their inner renewed heart-life. In short, he exhorts them not to masquerade in the garments of the world.

The word "conformed" in Rom. 8:29 is from *sunmorphoomai* which means "to bring to the same outward expression as something else, that outward expression proceeding from and being truly representative of one's true inward nature." The saints are predestined to be brought to the same outward expression as that which now is true of the Lord Jesus. He in His glorified humanity gives outward expression of His radiant beauty of character as the spotless, sinless, wonderful Son of God. The saints glorified will have an outward expression like that of the Lord Jesus, which expression proceeds from and is truly representative of their divine natures. The same word is used in Phil. 3:10 where it is translated "made conformable to." Paul's desire was that he would be brought to the place where he would become, both as to his inner heart life and also as to the outward expression of the same, like his Lord in His life of death to self and service to others.

GODHEAD. This word appears three times in the New Testament, Acts 17:29; Rom. 1:20; and Col. 2:9. The one word "Godhead" is the translation of two Greek words which have a real distinction between them, a distinction that grounds itself on their different derivations. In Rom. 1:20 we have the word *theiotes*. In this word, Trench says that "Paul is declaring how much of God may be known from the revelation of Himself which He has made in nature, from those vestiges of Himself which men may everywhere trace in the world around them. Yet it is not the personal God whom any man may learn to know by these aids: He can be known only by the revelation of Himself in His Son; but only His divine attributes, His majesty and glory. . . . . and it is not to be doubted that St. Paul uses this vaguer, more abstract, and less personal word, just because he would affirm that men may know God's power and majesty, His *theia dunamis* (divine power) (II Pet. 1:3), from His works; but would *not* imply that they may know Himself from these, or from anything short of the revelation of His eternal Word. Motives not dissimilar induce him to use *to theion* rather than *ho theos* in addressing the Athenians on Mars' Hill (Acts 17:29) ."

In Rom. 1:20, Paul states that the invisible things of God, here, His eternal power and His *theiotes*, His divinity, namely, the fact that He is a Being having divine attributes, are clearly seen by man through the created universe. Man, reasoning upon the basis of the law of cause and effect, namely, that every effect demands an adequate cause, comes to the conclusion that the universe as an effect demands an adequate cause, and that adequate cause must be a Being having divine attributes. It was as the creator of the universe that fallen man knew God (v. 21). Perhaps the word "Godhead" is the best one-word translation of *theiotes* in Rom. 1:20. But the term must be explained as above for a proper exegesis of this passage. The same is true of Acts 17:29. When Paul speaks of all men as the offspring of God, he uses the word *theos* for "God," the word that implies full deity as Paul knows God. But when he speaks of the Greek's conception of God or of what they as pagans might conceive God to be, he uses *theiotes*, for the Greeks could, apart from the revelation of God in Christ, only know Him as a Being of divine attributes.

In Col. 2:9 *theotes* is used. Here Trench says, "Paul is declaring that in the Son there dwells all the fulness of absolute

Godhead; they were no mere rays of divine glory which gilded Him, lighting up His Person for a season and with splendor not His own; but He was, and is, absolute and perfect God; and the apostle uses *theotes* to express this essential and personal Godhead of the Son." Here the word "divinity" will not do, only the word "deity." It is well in these days of apostasy, to speak of the *deity* of the Lord Jesus, not using the word "divinity" when we are referring to the fact that He is Very God. Modernism believes in His divinity, but in a way different from the scriptural conception of the term. Modernism has the pantheistic conception of the deity permeating all things and every man. Thus divinity, it says, is resident in every human being. It was resident in Christ as in all men. The difference between the divinity of Christ and that of all other men, it says, is one of degree, not of kind. Paul never speaks of the divinity of Christ, only of His deity. Our Lord has divine attributes since He is deity, but that is quite another matter from the Modernistic conception.

WORLD. There are three Greek words in the New Testament translated by this one English word, *kosmos, aion,* and *oikoumene.* It should be obvious that if one is to arrive at a full-orbed interpretation of the passages where the word "world" is found, one must know which Greek word is used, and the distinctive meaning of that Greek word. A knowledge of how these words were used in classical Greek, will help us to better understand their use in the New Testament.

The basic meaning of *kosmos* was "order." It was used in such expressions as "to sit in order." It meant "good order, good behavior, decency, a set form or order." When used of state or national existence, it meant "order, government." It also meant "an ornament, decoration, dress," especially of women. It was used to refer to the universe from the fact of its perfect arrangement. It was used in this case as opposed to the Greek word *chaos* which was used by the Greeks of the first state of existence, the rude, unformed mass out of which the universe was made. It was used to signify also empty immeasurable space. The reader will note that the Greeks believed that the original state of the universe was one of chaos. This is in line with the theory of evolution and the nebular hypothesis, which latter theory has been exploded by scientists, and which former theory is still held to tenaciously by the scientific world despite the fact that all branches of scientific investigation have been thoroughly probed, but no adequate cause for evolution has been found. The theory of evolution found its inception in the thinking of the Greek philosophers from the sixth to the fourth centuries B.C., Aristotle being one of its outstanding exponents. *Kosmos* also was used to refer to the inhabitants of the earth.

The papyri give us illustrations of the use of *kosmos* in the ordinary conversation of the *koine* period. A manuscript of 9 B.C., refers to the birthday of Augustus the Roman emperor, as the beginning of good news to the world (*kosmos*). At the Isthmian games (A.D. 67), a proclamation of the freedom of the Greeks was made, and the emperor Nero was described as the ruler of all the world (*kosmos*). The word is found in a reference to a bride's trousseau in the sense of "adornment." In a manuscript of 113 B.C., there is a complaint against certain persons who "throwing off all restraint (*kosmos*), knocked down a street door!"[19]

Aion which comes from *aio* "to breathe," means "a space or period of time," especially "a lifetime, life." It is used of one's time of life, age, the age of man, an age, a generation. It also means "a long space of time, eternity, forever." Again, it was used of space of time clearly defined and marked out, an era, age, period of a dispensation.

As to *aion,* the papyri speak of a person led off to death, the literal Greek being "led off from *aion* life."[20] A report of a public meeting speaks of a cry that was uttered by the

---

19, 20 *Moulton and Milligan.*

crowd, namely, "The Emperors forever" (*aion*).[21] It is also found in the sense of "a period of life."

Oikoumene, the third word, made up of the Greek word for "home" (*oikos*) and the verb "to remain" (*meno*), referred in classical Greek to the inhabitated world, namely, that portion of the earth inhabited by the Greeks, as opposed to the rest of the inhabited earth where non-Greeks or barbarians lived. Later it was used to designate the entire Roman empire. At the accession of Nero, the proclamation referred to him in the words "and the expectation and hope of the world has been declared Emperor, the good genius of the world and source of all good things, Nero, has been declared Caesar."[22] It was thus a common designation of the Roman Empire in the papyri.

We come now to the New Testament usage of the words. Cremer has the following to say about *kosmos*: "*Kosmos* denotes the sum-total of what God has created (John 17:5, 21:25; Acts 17:24; Rom. 1:20; I Cor. 4:9)." The expression "since the beginning of the world" (Mt. 24:21), Cremer says, "involves a reference to the fact that the world is the abode of man, or that order of things within which humanity moves, of which man is the center. . . . This leads us to the more precise definition of the conception, . . . As *kosmos* is regarded as that order of things whose center is man, attention is directed chiefly to him, and *kosmos* denotes mankind within that order of things, humanity as it manifests itself in and through such an order (Mt. 18:7). . . . The way would thus seem sufficiently prepared for the usage which by *kosmos* denotes that order of things which is alienated from God, as manifested in and by the human race, in which mankind exists; in other words, humanity as alienated from God, and acting in opposition to Him and to His revelation."

After taking up the classical meanings of *aion,* Cremer says of this word: "*aion* may denote either the duration of a defi-

---

21, 22. *Moulton and Milligan.*

nite space of time, or the (unending) duration of time in general."

Trench, contending for the use of the word "world" as the proper translation of *kosmos*, and "age" as the correct rendering of *aion* says: "One must regret that, by this or some other device, our translators did not mark the difference between *kosmos*, the world contemplated under aspects of space, and *aion*, the same contemplated under aspects of time."

Taking up the usage of *aion* he says: "Thus signifying time, it comes presently to signify all which exists in the world under conditions of time; . . . and then, more ethically, the course and current of this world's affairs. But this course and current being full of sin, it is nothing wonderful that 'this *aion*' set over against 'that *aion*' (Mt. 12:32) acquires, like *kosmos*, an unfavorable meaning." "This *aion*" refers to this age in which man lives, marked by its sin and corruption, "that *aion* to come," to the Millennial Age where the Lord Jesus will reign on earth and rule with a rod of iron. The expression does not have reference to this life as contrasted to the life after death, but to two different ages on the earth. He cites Gal. 1:4, "Who gave Himself for our sins, that He might deliver us from this present evil *aion*." Trench says that *aion* means "the age, the spirit or genius of the age." He defines *aion* as "All that floating mass of thoughts, opinions, maxims, speculations, hopes, impulses, aims, aspirations, at any time current in the world, which it may be impossible to seize and accurately define, but which constitutes a most real and effective power, being the moral or immoral atmosphere which at every moment of our lives we inhale, again inevitably to exhale." He says "All this is included in the *aion*, which is, as Bengel has expressed it, the subtle informing spirit of the *kosmos*, or world of men who are living alienated and apart from God."

To summarize: The word *kosmos* is used to refer to the world system, wicked and alienated from God yet cultured, educated, powerful, outwardly moral at times, the system of which Satan is the head, the fallen angels and the demons are his servants, and all mankind other than the saved, are his subjects. This includes those people, pursuits, pleasures, purposes, and places where God is not wanted (Mt. 4:8; John 12:31; I John 2:15, 16, being examples). It refers also to the human race, fallen, totally depraved (John 3:16). It may have reference to the created universe (John 1:10 first and second mention). It may also refer simply to mankind without any particular reference to man's fallen and wicked condition (Gal. 4:3; Jas. 2:5). *Kosmos* is translated in every place by the word "world" except in I Pet. 3:3 where it is rendered "adornment." In interpreting the passages where *kosmos* is found, the student should study the context in order to determine which one of the above meanings is to be used in any particular passage.

Aion is translated "world" in the following places where the student would do better to translate it by the word "age," and apply the definition given above, interpreting the passage in the light of the context: Mt. 12:32, 13:22, 39, 40, 49, 24:3, 28:20; *Mk.* 4:19, 10:30; *Lk.* 1:70, 16:8, 18:30, 20:34, 35; *John* 9:32; *Acts* 3:21, 15:18; *Rom.* 12:2; *I Cor.* 1:20, 2:6, 7, 8, 3:18, 10:11; *II Cor.* 4:4; *Gal.* 1:4; *Eph.* 1:21, 2:2, 3:9, 3:21, 6:12; *I Tim.* 6:17; *II Tim.* 4:10; *Tit.* 2:12; *Heb.* 1:2, 6:5, 9:26, 11:3.

In *Luke* 1:70; *John* 9:32; *Acts* 3:21, 15:18; *Eph.* 3:9, 3:21, the word is used to specify time as such, and does not have its usual meaning of a period of time characterized by a certain spirit or way of life, for instance Luke 1:70, "which have been since time began" (lit., "from ever"). In Hebrews 1:2 and 11:3 the word refers to the created universe and the periods of time as administered by God. *Aion* is translated "course" in Ephesians 2:2 where "world" is from *kosmos*.

Oikoumene is found in *Mt.* 24:14; *Lk.* 2:1, 4:5, 21:26; *Acts* 11:28, 17:6, 31, 19:27, 24:5; *Rom.* 10:18; *Heb.* 1:6, 2:5; *Rev.* 3:10, 12:9, 16:14.

Kosmos occurs so often that we cannot list the places in a brief work like this. The student can check with the places where *aion* and *oikoumene* are found. If the scripture is not listed there, *kosmos* is in the Greek text of the passage under consideration.

WORD. The Lord Jesus is called THE WORD in John 1:1, 14; I John 1:1, 5:7; Rev. 19:13. In John 1:1 we have the preexistence of the Word, His fellowship with God the Father in His preincarnate state, and His absolute deity. In John 1:14 the incarnation of the Word is in view. I John 1:1 speaks of the things which the disciples heard and saw with reference to the earthly life of the Word. In I John 5:7, the name "The Word" is used as a designation of our Lord in connection with the names *Father* and *Spirit*. In Rev. 19:13 the descending Conqueror is called The Word.

The purpose of this study is to ascertain the meaning and usage of the Greek word *logos* which is translated *word* in these passages, and thus come to understand its significance when used as a name of our Lord.

In classical Greek *logos* meant "the word or outward form by which the inward thought is expressed and made known," or "the inward thought or reason itself." *Logos* never meant in classical Greek a word in the grammatical sense as the mere name of a thing, but rather the thing referred to, the material, not the formal part. It also referred to the power of the mind which is manifested in speech, also to the reason. For instance, it is found in the phrase, "agreeably to reason." It meant "examination by reason, reflection," as opposed to "thoughtlessness, rashness." It is used in the phrase "to allow himself reflection." It was used in the sense of the esteem or regard one may have for another. The word is found in the phrase, "to be of no account or repute with one;" also in the phrase, "to make one of account;" also in the phrase "to make account," that is, to put a value on a person or thing. These classical uses of *logos* provide us with a background and basis upon which to study its New Testament usage.

Cremer commences his discussion of *logos* by stating the fact that the Greek language has three words, *hrema, onoma,* and *epos* which designate a word in its grammatical sense, a function which *logos* does not have. He says that *logos* is used of the living spoken word, "the word not in its outward form, but with reference to the thought connected with the form, . . . in short, not the word of language, but of conversation, of discourse; not the word as a part of speech, but the word as part of what is uttered."

Cremer finds the Johannine usage of *logos* as a name of the Lord Jesus to be in "perfect accord with the progress of God's gracious revelation in the Old Testament," and that "John's use of the term is the appropriate culmination of the view presented in other parts of the N.T., of the word of God, denoting . . . the mystery of Christ." He says that the term "the word of the Lord" in the O.T., refers to the Lord Jesus in His preincarnate state. In Jer. 1:4, 5, we have, "Then the Word of the Lord came unto me, saying, Before I formed thee in the belly I knew thee." Two acts which clearly imply personality, *forming* and *knowing,* are predicated of the Word of the Lord. Cremer quotes Neuman on Jer. 1:2 as follows; "The word of God, the self-revelation of the eternal Godhead from eternity in the Word, is the source and principle of all prophetic words; therein they have their divine basis." He states that the Aramaic paraphrase of Numbers 7:89 according to the Targums is, "The Word spoke with him from off the mercy seat." Cremer says, "God Himself is the word insofar as the word is the medium of His revelation of Himself, and the word, though personality and hypostasis are not yet attributed to it, occupies a middle place between God and man. . . . That this representation was included in the Jewish idea of the Messiah, is clear from Gen. 49:18 where the Jerusalem Targum has, 'I have waited, not for liberation through Sampson or Gideon, but for salvation through Thy Word.' "

This O.T., foregleam of the Lord Jesus as The Word, comes to full expression in the *Logos* of John in the N.T. The Lord Jesus in John's writings is the *Logos* in that He is "the representative and expression of what God has to say to the world, in whom and by whom God's mind and purposes towards the world find their expression" (*Cremer*).

The word *logos* was already in use among the Greeks before John used it. It was used to denote the principle which maintains order in the world. In connection with the Greek word for "seed" in its adjective form, it was used to express the generative principle or creative force in nature. The term was familiar to Greek philosophy. The word thus being already in use, among the Hebrews in a biblical way, and among the Greeks in a speculative and rather hazy, undefined way, John now proceeds to unfold the true nature of the Logos, Jesus Christ. Vincent quotes Godet as saying in this connection, "To those Hellenists and Hellenistic Jews, on the one hand, who were vainly philosophizing on the relations of the finite and infinite; to those investigators of the letter of the Scriptures, on the other, who speculated about the theocratic revelations, John said, by giving this name Logos to Jesus: 'The unknown Mediator between God and the world, the knowledge of whom you are striving after, we have seen, heard, and touched. Your philosophical speculations and your scriptural subtleties will never raise you to Him. Believe as we do in Jesus, and you will possess in Him that divine Revealer who engages your thoughts'."

Vincent says, "As Logos has the double meaning of *thought* and *speech,* so Christ is related to God as the word to the idea, the word being not merely a *name* for the idea, but the idea itself expressed." He quotes the following from William Austin; "The name *Word* is most excellently given to our

Saviour; for it expresses His nature in one, more than in any others. Therefore St. John, when he names the Person in the Trinity (1 John 5:7), chooses rather to call Him *Word* than *Son;* for *word* is a phrase more communicable than *son. Son* hath only reference to the *Father* that begot Him; but *word* may refer to him that *conceives* it; to him that *speaks* it; to *that which is spoken by* it; to *the voice* that it is clad in; and to the effects it raises in him that hears it. So Christ, as He is *the Word,* not only refers to His Father that begot Him, and from whom He comes forth, but to all the creatures that were made by Him; to the flesh that He took to clothe Him; and to the doctrine He brought and taught, and which lives yet in the hearts of all them that obediently do hear it. He it is that is *this Word;* and any other, prophet or preacher, he is but *a voice* (Luke 3:4). *Word* is *an inward conception of the mind;* and *voice* is but *a sign of intention.* St. John was but a sign, a *voice;* not worthy to untie the shoe-latchet of this Word. Christ is the *inner conception* 'in the bosom of His Father;' and that is properly *the Word.* And yet the Word is the intention uttered forth, as well as conceived within; for Christ was no less the Word in the womb of the Virgin, or in the cradle of the manger, or on the altar of the cross, than He was in the beginning, 'in the bosom of His Father.' For as the intention departs not from the mind when the word is uttered, so Christ, proceeding from the Father by eternal generation, and after here by birth and incarnation, remains still in Him and with Him in essence; as the intention, which is conceived and born in the mind, remains still with it and in it, though the word be spoken. He is therefore rightly called *the Word,* both by His coming from, and yet remaining still in, the Father."

DWELL.[23] This word in John 1:14; Rev. 7:15, 21:3, is the translation in these places of *skenoo* which means "to live in

---

23. *Limited.*

a tent," the Greek word for "tent" being *skene*. In John 1:14, we have, "the Word *became* (*ginomai*) flesh, and lived in a tent among us." That tent was His physical body. Paul speaks of our present physical body as a *skene*, a tent (II Cor. 5:1). In Rev. 7:15, 21:3, the Lord Jesus is seen in the body of His glory, dwelling in the same tent He lived in while on earth, but in that tent glorified. God the Son will live in that tent, His glorified human body, all through eternity, with the saved of the human race, who like Him will live in their earthly tents glorified.

VILE.[24] This is the translation of *tapeinonis* (Phil. 3:21). The same Greek word is used in Lk. 1:48 where it is translated "low estate," in Acts 8:33 where it is rendered "humiliation," and in Jas. 1:10, where we have "is made low." Our present physical bodies have been humiliated, made low, brought to a low condition by the fall of Adam. They have the sin principle indwelling them. They are mortal bodies subject to sickness, weariness, and death.

ABIDE.[25] This is one of John's favorite words. The Greek word is *meno*. Its classical usage will throw light upon the way it is used in the N.T. It meant "to stay, stand fast, abide, to stay at home, stay where one is, not stir, to remain as one was, to remain as before." In the N.T., it means "to sojourn, to tarry, to dwell at one's own house, to tarry as a guest, to lodge, to maintain unbroken fellowship with one, to adhere to his party, to be constantly present to help one, to put forth constant influence upon one." "In the mystic phraseology of John, God is said to *meno* in Christ, i.e., to dwell as it were in Him, to be continually operative in Him by His divine influence and energy (John 14:10); Christians are said to *meno* in God, to be rooted as it were in Him, knit to Him by the Spirit they have received from Him (I John 2:6, 24, 27, 3:6);

24, 25. *Limited.*

hence one is said to *meno* in Christ or in God, and conversely, Christ or God is said to *meno* in one (John 6:56, 15:4) ."[26] Thayer quotes Ruckert in the use of *meno* in the words "Something has established itself permanently within my soul, and always exerts its power in me."

The word therefore has the ideas of "permanence of position, occupying a place as one's dwelling place, holding and maintaining unbroken communion and fellowship with another." John uses *meno* in the following places; in the Gospel, 1:32, 33, 38, 39, 2:12, 3:36, 4:40, 5:38, 6:27, 56, 7:9, 8:31, 35, 9:41, 10:40, 11:6, 12:24, 34, 12:46, 14:10, 16, 17, 25, 15:4, 5, 6, 7, 9, 10, 11, 16, 19:31, 21:22, 23; in the First Epistle, 2:6, 10, 14, 17, 19, 24, 27, 28, 3:6, 9, 14, 15, 17, 24, 4:12, 13, 15, 16; in the Second Epistle, 2, 9. The words "abide, dwell, tarry, continue, be present," are the various translations in the A.V. Study these places where the word occurs, and obtain a comprehensive view of its usage.

In John 15, the abiding of the Christian in Christ refers to his maintaining unbroken fellowship with Him. *He makes his spiritual home in Christ.* There is nothing between himself and his Saviour, no sin unjudged and not put away. He depends upon Him for spiritual life and vigor as the branch is dependent upon the vine. The abiding of Christ in the Christian is His permanent residence in Him and His supplying that Christian with the necessary spiritual energy to produce fruit in his life through the ministry of the Holy Spirit.

COMING.[27] This word is the translation of *parousia* which is made up of the word *para* meaning "beside" and the participial form of the verb "to be," the compound word meaning literally "being beside."

In classical Greek it meant "a being present, the presence of a person or a thing, especially the presence of a person for

26. *Thayer.*
27. *Limited.*

the purpose of assisting, the arrival of a person." It was used of one's substance or property. From the papyri, Moulton and Milligan report the following; "the repair of what has been swept away by the river requires my presence." They report its usage in the quasi-technical force of "a 'visit' of a king, emperor, or other person of authority, the official character of the 'visit' being further emphasized by the taxes or payments that were exacted to make preparations for it." They say that in popular usage it had the general sense of "arrival" or "presence."

There is another word translated "coming" (*erchomai*), which refers to the movement of a person from one place to another, and means "to go or to come." This is used, for instance in Mt. 16:28 in the words "till they see the Son of Man coming in His kingdom." Here the emphasis is, not upon His arrival or personal presence, but upon His coming from heaven to earth. *Parousia* is used in the following scriptures: *Mt.* 24:3, 27, 37, 39; *I Cor.* 15:23, 16:17; *II Cor.* 7:6, 7, 10:10; *Phil* 1:26, 2:12; *I Thes.* 2:19, 3:13, 4:15, 5:23; *II Thes.* 2:1, 8, 9; *Jas.* 5:7, 8; *II Pet.* 1:16, 3:4, 12; *I John* 2:28. When the word is used of the Lord Jesus, it means "a royal visit," but when it refers to Paul for instance it merely refers to his personal presence.

CONVERSATION. There are three Greek words translated by the one English word "conversation." Today this word means discourse between individuals. In 1611 A.D., when the Authorized Version was translated, it meant what the Greek words mean of which it is the translation. We have a two-fold purpose therefore in our study, first, to find out what these three words meant in general, and second, to inquire into the shades of meaning between them so that we can arrive at a clearer, more accurate understanding and interpretation of the passages where each occurs.

The first word we will study is *anastrophe* (the noun), and *anastrepho* (the verb). In classical Greek, the verb meant among other things "to turn one's self about, to turn back, round, or about, to dwell in a place," the noun, "a turning back or about, occupation in a thing, a mode of life, behaviour." One can see that the ideas of "a mode of life" and "one's behaviour" are derived from the fact of one's activity.

Thayer's note is helpful. He says that the verb means "to conduct or behave one's self, to walk," the latter meaning not referring here to the physical act of walking but to the act of determining our course of conduct and the carrying out of that determined course of action. The noun means "one's walk, manner of life, conduct." In the biblical use of the word, the moral and spiritual aspect of one's manner of life is in view. The noun *anastrophe* is found in *Gal.* 1:13; *Eph.* 4:22; *I Tim.* 4:12; *Heb.* 13:7; *Jas.* 3:13; *I Pet.* 1:15, 18, 2:12, 3:1, 2, 16; *II Pet.* 2:77, 3:11; the verb in *II Cor.* 1:12; *Eph.* 2:3.

The second word is *politeuomai* (the verb) (Phil. 1:27), and *politeuma* (the noun) (Phil. 3:20). The word occurs only here in the N.T. In classical Greek, the verb meant "to be a citizen or a freeman, to live in a free state, to be a free citizen, to live as a free citizen." The noun meant "citizenship, life as a citizen." Here are two words which Paul uses in their original classical meaning. Philippi was a Roman colony. Its citizens therefore were citizens of the Roman empire. Roman citizenship carried with it great privileges and honors, also great responsibilities.

Paul is speaking of the Christian lives of the Philippian saints, their manner of life and their behavior. He could have used the words *"anastrepho"* and *"anastrophe"* which we found so frequently in the N.T. But because the Philippian church was located in a city that was a Roman colony, he had the opportunity of using a more specialized word. The first two words refer to conduct as such. Our present two words refer to conduct as related to one's position as a citizen of a commonwealth. The citizen of Philippi was not only obligated to order his manner of life in the right manner. He was not merely obligated to do what he thought was right. He was to govern his conduct so that it would conform to what Rome would expect of him. He had responsibilities and duties which inhered in his position as a citizen of Rome. Thus, our second two words are an advance upon the first two in that while the former in their context speak of behaviour that is good or bad as the case might be, the latter refer to conduct that is measured by a standard. Paul uses the second word in the Philippian epistle, to teach the Philippians that they were also citizens of heaven, and as such, their conduct must be governed by a standard, that of heaven. They are to live a heavenly life, for they were a colony of heaven on earth.

The third word is *tropos*. It is translated just once in the N.T., by the word "conversation" (Heb. 13:5). The word comes from *trepo* which means "to turn or guide towards a thing, to turn one's self, to direct one's attention to a thing, to be occupied with it." Thus *tropos* comes to mean "manner of life, behavior."

HARPAZO. This is a Greek word which has various meanings. It is not translated by one uniform English word. The meanings are as follows: "to seize, to carry off by force, to claim for one's self eagerly, to snatch out or away." It was used proverbially in the sense of "to rescue from the danger of destruction." It was used also of divine power transferring a person marvellously and swiftly from one place to another.

The word is used in *Mt.* 11:12, 13:19; *John* 6:15, 10:12, 28, 29; *Acts* 8:39, 23:10; *II Cor.* 12:2, 4; *I Thes.* 4:17; *Jude* 23; Rev. 12:5. The procedure in Greek exegesis when a word has a number of meanings, is to use only those meanings which are in accord with the context. For instance, in the case of *harpazo* in its use in connection with the wolf (John 10:12), it would not do to interpret it in the sense of rescuing from the danger of destruction. It would mean here "to seize and carry off by force, to claim for one's self eagerly." Study these places where the word occurs, using as many meanings as agree with the context. Pay especial attention to I Thes. 4:17, and see how much new truth you obtain regarding the Rapture of the Church.

QUICKEN. We must not make the mistake of thinking that this word refers to the act of energizing something or someone already alive. The Greeks had a word for that. It is the word *energeo*, from which we get our words "energy," and "energize." The word *energeo* is used in Eph. 2:2 where demonic activity is said to be working in (*energeo*), energizing the unsaved. It is used in Phil. 2:13, where God is said to be energizing the saved. *Energeo* means "to be operative, to be at work, to put forth power." This activity put forth in an individual energizes him to the doing of certain things intended by the one who is doing the energizing.

The word translated "quicken" namely, *zoopoieo* does not mean "to energize." It is made up of one of the Greek words for life, *zoe*, which refers to the life principle in contradistinction to *bios* which refers to that which sustains life, and the word *poieo* which means "to make." This verb in classical Greek meant "to produce animals," used especially of worms and grubs. The noun meant " a making alive, a bringing to life," the adjective, "able to make alive, generating power." This is the genius of the word. It is so used in the N.T. Moulton and Milligan say that the word was used as a frequent attribute of the Trinity in the late papyri. They give an extract of the sixth century A.D., from which we offer the following translation; "in the name of the One who is holy and who makes alive and who is of the same substance, the Three, Father, Son, and Holy Spirit."

Study this word in the following scriptures: *John* 5:21, 6:63; *Rom.* 4:17, 8:11; *I Cor.* 15:22, 36, 45; *II Cor.* 3:6; *Gal.* 3:21;

I Tim. 6:13; *I Pet.* 3:18. In some places the word is translated "be made alive" etc. To make alive or to give life presupposes a state of death. For instance, Rom. 8:11 does not refer to the Holy Spirit energizing or animating the physical body of the saint during this life, but to the act of giving life to that body after it has died. The verse refers to the future resurrection of the saints. The word "quick" thus means "alive," as in Heb. 4:12, "The word of God is alive and powerful (*energes*) ." Here we have the Greek word "alive" used in connection with the word which means "energy," demonstrating that the two words have a distinct meaning of their own.

BAPTIZE, BAPTISM. These two words are not native to the English language. Therefore, they do not have any intrinsic meaning of their own. The only rightful meaning they can have is the one that is derived from the Greek word of which they are the spelling. The verb is spelled *baptizo*, from which with a slight change in spelling we get our word "baptize." The noun is *baptisma*, and taking off the last letter, we have "baptism."

We will study these words first in their classical usage. The word *baptizo* is related to another Greek word *bapto*. The latter meant "to dip, dip under." It was used of the smith tempering the red-hot steel. It was used also in the sense of "to dip in dye, to colour, to steep." It was used of the act of dyeing the hair, and of glazing earthen vessels. It was used as a proverb in the sense of "steeping someone in crimson," that is, giving him a bloody coxcomb. It meant also "to fill by dipping in, to draw." It was used of a ship that dipped, that is, sank. *Baptizo*, the related word meant "to dip repeatedly." It was used of the act of sinking ships. It meant also "to bathe." It was used in the phrase "soaked in wine," where the word "soaked" is the meaning of *baptizo*. It is found in the phrase "overhead and ears in debt," where the

words "overhead and ears" are the graphic picture of what
the word meant. The word here means therefore "complete-
ly submerged." Our present day English equivalent would be
"sunk." A *baptes* is one who dips or dyes. A *baptisis* is a
dipping, bathing, a washing, a drawing of water. A *baptisma*
is that which is dipped. A *baptisterion* is a bathing place, a
swimming bath. A *baptistes* is one that dips, a dyer. *Baptos*
means "dipped, dyed, bright colored, drawn like water."

Baptizo is used in the ninth book of the Odyssey, where the
hissing of the burning eye of the Cyclops is compared to the
sound of water where a smith dips (*baptizo*) a piece of iron,
tempering it. In the Battle of the Frogs and Mice, it is said
that a mouse thrust a frog with a reed, and the frog leaped
over the water, (*baptizo*) dyeing it with his blood. Euripedes
uses the word of a ship which goes down in the water and
does not come back to the surface. Lucian dreams that he has
seen a huge bird shot with a mighty arrow, and as it flies high
in the air, it dyes (*baptizo*) the clouds with his blood. An
ancient scholium to the Fifth Book of the Iliad makes a
wounded soldier dye (*baptizo*) the earth with his blood. In
Xenophon's Anabasis, we have the instance where the Greek
soldiers placed (*baptizo*) the points of their spears in a bowl
of blood.

We come now to the usage of these words in Koine Greek,
giving examples from the papyri, the LXX, and the New
Testament.

In secular documents of the Koine period, Moulton and
Milligan report the following uses of *baptizo*, "a *submerged*
boat, ceremonial *ablutions,* a person *flooded* or *overwhelmed*
in calamities." They say that the word was used in its metaphorical sense even among uneducated people. A biblical
example of this use is found in our Lord's speaking of His
Passion as a "baptism" (Mk. 10:38). These scholars report
the use of *bapto* as referring to fullers and dyers. The word
is used of colored garments, and of wool to be dyed. The word

baptisma is found in a question regarding a new baptism someone is reported to be preaching. This use of this noun is peculiar to the N.T., and to ecclesiastical writers.

In the LXX we have in Leviticus 4:6 the words, "And the priest shall dip (*bapto*) his finger in the blood, and sprinkle (*prosraino*) of the blood seven times before the Lord." Here the word *bapto* is found in juxtaposition to *prosraino*, a verb closely allied to *prosrantizo*, *bapto* meaning "to dip," the latter verb "to sprinkle."

In the N.T., we have the rich man asking that Lazarus dip (*bapto*) his finger in water and cool his tongue (Luke 16:24). In Heb. 9:10 *baptisma* is translated "washings" and refers to the ceremonial ablutions of Judaism. In Mk. 7:4 *baptisma* is used of the ceremonial washing of cups, pots, brazen vessels, and tables. *Baptisma* is used in Mt. 3:7, and *baptizo* in Mt. 3:16, and I Cor. 1:14, of the rite of water baptism. In Mk. 10:38 our Lord speaks of His sufferings on the Cross as the *baptisma* with which He is to be *baptizo*.

In these examples of the various uses of the words *bapto* and *baptizo* we discover three distinct usages, a *mechanical* one, a *ceremonial* one, and a *metaphorical* one.

The *mechanical* usage can be illustrated by the action of the smith dipping the hot iron in water, tempering it, or the dyer dipping the cloth in the dye for the purpose of dying it. These instances of the use of our Greek word, give us the following definition of the word in its mechanical usage. The word refers to the introduction or placing of a person or thing into a new environment or into union with something else so as to alter its condition or its relationship to its previous environment or condition. While the word, we found, had other uses, yet the one that predominated above the others was the above one. Observe how perfectly this meaning is in accord with the usage of the word in Romans 6:3, 4, where the believing sinner is baptized into vital union with Jesus Christ. The believing sinner is introduced or placed in Christ, thus coming into union with Him. By that action he is taken out of his old environment and condition in which he had lived, the First Adam, and is placed into a new environment and condition, the Last Adam. By this action his condition is changed from that of a lost sinner with a totally depraved nature to that of a saint with a divine nature. His relationship to the law of God is changed from that of a guilty sinner to that of a justified saint. All this is accomplished by the act of the Holy Spirit introducing or placing him into vital union with Jesus Christ. *No ceremony of water baptism ever did that.* The entire context is supernatural in its character. The Greek word here should not be transliterated but translated, and the translation should read; "As many as were introduced (placed) into Christ Jesus, into His death were introduced. Therefore we were buried with Him through the aforementioned introduction into His death." The same holds true of I Cor. 12:13 which should be translated, "For through the instrumentality of one Spirit were we all placed into one body." It is because we so often associate the English word "baptism" with the rite of water baptism, that we read that ceremony into Romans 6. A student is one of the writer's Greek classes who is a Greek himself, who learned to speak that language as his mother tongue and studied it in the schools of Greece, stated during a class discussion that the Greek reader would react to the Greek text of Romans and the word *baptizo* as the writer has. The purely mechanical usage of our word is seen in the following places: Mt. 3:11 (second occurrence); Mk. 1:8 (second); Luke 3:6 (second), 16:24; John 1:33 (second), 13:26; Acts 1:5 (second), 11:16 (second); Rom. 6:3, 4; I Cor. 12:13; Gal. 3:27; Eph. 4:5; Col. 2:12; Rev. 19:13.

Before listing the places where the word occurs in its ceremonial usage, we will trace the usage of *baptizo* back to Levitical washings. In the LXX (Lev. 14: 8, 9, 15:5, 6, 7, 8, 10, 11, 16, 18, 21, 22, 27, 17:15, 15:13, 16:4, 24, 28) the word "wash" is *louo*. This Greek word is found in Acts 22:16 in connection with the word *baptizo* in the expression, "Be baptized and wash away thy sins." According to Mk. 7:4 "washing of cups" (*baptizo*), Lk. 11:38, and Heb. 9:10, where *baptizo* is used, that word seems to have been the technical term at the time for these washings. Expressions like those in Isaiah 1:16, and the prophecies like those in Ezek. 36:25, 37:23, and Zech. 13:1 are connected with the Levitical washings. These washings and the prophecies are connected with the purification which followed the act of expiation or cleansing from sin (Ex. 19:14; Lev. 13:14; Heb. 10:22, 23). Thus, that which the word *baptizo* stood for was not unknown to the Jews. While the ceremonial washings of Leviticus were performed by the person himself, with one exception, and that was where Moses in installing Aaron and his sons as priests, himself washed them (Lev. 8:6), John *baptizo* his converts himself.

Baptizo in the ministry of our Lord and John was, like the theocratic washings and purifications, a symbol whose design was to point to the purging away of sin on whom the rite was performed (Mt. 3:6; John 3:22-25). John's baptism was in response to the repentance of the individual (Mt. 3:11). It was connected with his message of an atonement for sin that was to be offered in the future, and the necessity of faith in that atonement (Acts 19:4).

John's baptism had looked ahead to a coming Saviour. Paul's baptism, or Christian baptism now looks back to a Saviour who has died and who has arisen again (Acts 19:5). That the rite of water baptism is the outward testimony of the inward fact of a person's salvation, and that it follows his act of receiving Christ as Saviour and is not a prerequisite to his receiving salvation, is seen in the use of the preposition *eis* in Mt. 3:11 where the translation should read, "I indeed baptize you with water because of repentance." While the act of Christian baptism is a testimony of the person that his

sins have been washed away, it also pictures and symbolizes
the fact of the believing sinner's identification with Christ
in His death, burial, and resurrection (Rom. 6:), for *baptizo*
means, "to dip, to immerse." It never means "to sprinkle."
The Greeks had a word for "sprinkle" namely, *rantizo*. The
two words, *baptizo* and *rantizo* are used in juxtaposition in
Lev. 4:6.

The following are the places where *baptizo* is used of the
baptism administered by John the Baptist and by the disciples
of our Lord under the dispensation of law. *Mt.* 3:6, 11:1 (first
mention), 13, 14, 16; *Mk.* 1:4, 5, 8 (first mention), 9; *Lk.* 3:7,
12, 16 (first mention), 21, 7:29, 30; *John* 1:25, 26, 28, 31, 33
(first mention), 3:22, 23, 26, 4:1, 2, 10:40; *Acts* 1:5, (first
mention) 11:16 (first mention), 19:4 (first mention). The
noun *baptisma* when it is used of the baptism in the dispensation of law is found in the following places: *Mt.* 3:7, 21:25;
Mk. 1:4, 11:30; *Lk.* 3:3, 7:29, 20:4; *Acts* 1:22, 10:37, 13:24,
18:25, 19:34.

The word *baptizo* is used of the ablutions of the Jews
which were extra-Biblical, and which were called the tradi-
tions of the elders (*Mt.* 15:2), in *Mk.* 7:4, *Lk.* 11:38. The
noun *baptismos* is used in connection with the same prac-
tices in Mt. 7:4; Mk. 7:8. It is used of the Levitical ablutions
in Heb. 6:2, 9:10.

Baptizo is used of Christian baptism in *Mt.* 28:19; *Acts* 2:38,
41, 8:12, 13, 16, 36, 38, 9:18, 10:47, 48, 16:15, 33, 18:8, 19:5,
22:16; *I Cor.* 1:13, 14, 15, 16, 17, 15:29. *Baptisma* is used in
I Pet. 3:21 of Christian baptism.

The metaphorical use of *baptizo* we find in Mt. 20:22, 23;
Mk. 10:38, 39; Lk. 12:50. A metaphor is the use of a word
or phrase literally denoting one kind of object or idea in
place of another by way of suggesting a likeness or analogy
between them, for example, "the ship *plows* the sea." In the
above passages, our Lord is speaking of His sufferings in connection with the Cross. He speaks of them as a baptism. The

words were uttered while He was on His way to Jerusalem to be crucified. John the Baptist had announced His coming and had baptized the multitudes. Our Lord's disciples had been baptizing during the three years of His ministry. The words *baptizo* and *baptisma* which are used by Matthew, Mark, and Luke had by that time become the technical and common Greek words used to describe the rite administered by John and our Lord's disciples. Our Lord used the rite of baptism as a metaphor to speak of His coming sufferings. Just as a convert was plunged into the baptismal waters, He was about to be plunged into His sufferings. Just as the person would be immersed in the water, so He would be overwhelmed by His sufferings. Just as the person would come up out of the water, so He would be freed from His sufferings and arise from the dead.

There is one passage in which *baptizo* is found that we have not classified. It is I Cor. 10:2 "were all baptized unto Moses." *Expositor's Greek Testament* has an illuminating note on it. " 'The cloud' shading and guiding the Israelites from above, and the 'sea' making a path for them through the midst and drowning their enemies behind them, were glorious signs to 'our fathers' of God's salvation; together they formed a washing of regeneration (Tit. 3:5), inaugurating the national life; as it trode the miraculous path between upper and nether waters, Israel was born into its Divine estate. Thus 'they all received their baptism *unto Moses* in the cloud and in the sea' since in this act they committed themselves to the guidance of Moses, entering through him into acknowledged fellowship with God."

AIR. The Greeks had two words which meant "air," *aer* and *aither*. *Aer* was used to designate the lower air, the thick air or haze that surrounds the earth. *Aither* was the name given the pure, upper air as opposed to the thick lower air. The pure upper air started at the mountain tops for the

Greeks of the ancient world, since they had no way of exploring the regions above these.

The word *aer*, referring to the lower atmosphere, namely, that below the mountain tops, is used in the N.T. *Aither* is not used, although it must have been in common use in the first century. One can understand the use of this word as that which would naturally be expected in such scriptures as Acts 22:23; I Cor. 9:26, 14:9; Rev. 9:2, 16:17. But it gives one pause to see it used in Eph. 2:2 and I Thes. 4:17. Study these latter two scriptures in the light of the particular meaning of the word *aer*.

ADOPTION. This word is the translation of *huiothesia*, a word made up of *huios* "a son," and *thesia*, a form of the verb *tithemi* meaning "to place," the compound word meaning "to place as a son." The Greek word *teknon* which means "a child," comes from the verb *tikto* "to give birth to." It therefore has in it the idea of birth relationship. The word means "a born-one." The word *huios* does not have this implication. *Huios* is used in Gal. 3:26 of the believer under grace as opposed to the believer under law. The latter was under the schoolmaster (the *paidagogos*), a slave charged with the moral supervision of a child in its minority. The word *teknon* is used in Galatians (4:25, 27, 28, 31) of the believer under law. Thus a *teknon* is a believer in his minority, a *huios*, an adult son. Believers under the covenant of law were *teknon*, that is born children of God in their minority. Believers under grace, are both *teknon*, born children of God and *huios*, adult sons of God. This meaning of an adult son is to be used only where the word refers to a believer in this age of grace. The word is used also in the N.T., as a Hebrew idiom, where a person having a peculiar quality, or is subject to a peculiar evil, is called the son, (*huios*) of that quality (Lk. 10:6, Eph. 2:2, 5:6, 8). The word *huios* is also used to refer to the male issue or child.

The A.V., uniformly translates *teknon* by the word "child" except in the following places where it is rendered by the word "son," which is the proper translation of *huios*. *Mt.* 9:2, 21:28; *Mk.* 2:5, 13:12; *Lk.* 2:48, 15:31, 16:25; *John* 1:12; *I Cor.* 4:14, 17; *Phil.* 2:15, 22; *I Tim.* 1:2, 18; *II Tim.* 1:2, 2:1; *Tit.* 1:4; *Phm.* 10; *I John* 3:1, 2. Study these passages, using the word "child" in the translation, keeping in mind the idea of the birth-relationship existing, and see what clearer light is thrown upon them. For instance, Mary calls Jesus "child." He was only twelve years old at the time. Yet this child was confuting the learned Doctors (Lk. 2:48). Timothy was Paul's child and the latter was his spiritual father, for Paul had won Timothy to the Lord. In John 1:12, regeneration is in view. In I John 3:1, 2, the fact that we are born-children of God, is in view, having the nature of God. In Phil. 2:15, believers, being children of God, and possessing therefore the nature of God, are expected to reflect in their lives the holiness, love, and other qualities of God.

The word *huios* is uniformly translated "son" except in certain places, some of which rightfully use the word "children" where the plural refers to children of both sexes. But the following places should be translated by the word "son": *Mt.* 23:15; *Lk.* 6:35, 16:8, 20:34, 36; *John* 12:36; *Acts* 3:25, 13:10; *Rom.* 9:26; *Gal.* 3:26; *Eph.* 2:2, 5:6; *Col.* 3:6; *I Thes.* 5:5. It will be observed that in many of the above places the Hebrew idiom is used where a person having a peculiar quality or is subject to a peculiar evil, is called the son (*huios*) of that quality or evil. He partakes of the nature of that quality.

Coming now to the word "adoption" (*huiothesia*), we find that it was a term used in Roman legal practice. It referred to a legal action by which a person takes into his family a child not his own, with the purpose of treating him as and giving him all the privileges of an own son. The custom was not common among the Jews, but was so among the Romans, with whom an adopted child is legally entitled to all rights and privileges of a natural-born child. This custom, well-known in the Roman empire, is used in the N.T., as an illustration of the act of God giving a believing sinner, who is not His natural child, a position as His adult son in His family. This is a legal act and position, and not the same as regeneration and a place in the family as a born-child of God.

The word is found in *Rom.* 8:15, 23, 9:4; *Gal.* 4:5; *Eph.* 1:5. In Rom. 8:15 it is the Holy Spirit who places believing sinners in the family of God as adult sons. In Rom. 8:23, believers have already been placed in the family of God, and are led by the Spirit as the adult sons of God. But only when their mortal bodies have been glorified at the Rapture, will they possess all that sonship involves. In Rom. 9:4, the nation Israel is said to have been placed in the special relationship as the peculiar people of God, thus God's own by adoption. Gal. 4:5 and Eph. 1:5 refer to the same thing that Rom. 8:15 refers to.

ACCESS is the translation of *prosagoge,* a word made up of the verb *ago* which means "to go," and the preposition *pros* which means "toward, facing." The word is used in Rom. 5:2, Eph. 2:18, 3:12. In the papyri the word was used in the technical sense of "a landing stage." It is thought that it was used as a nautical term of the approach of a ship to a haven or harbor where it could land. Thus the total idea in the word would be access into and rest in a haven or harbor. In the case of Rom. 5:2, God's grace is there pictured as a haven for the soul. The word "have" is perfect tense in Greek. Thus the words "have access" speak of a permanent haven for the soul.

The verb *prosago,* which is the base of the word translated "access," means in its intransitive use, "approach, a drawing near." Thus our word speaks not only of a haven of rest and security, but of a drawing near to God. The word *prosago* means also "to bring into the presence of," thus "to present, to introduce." It is found in the sentence, "Cronion, who now happens to be in Alexandria, will bring them before his highness the high-priest."[28] It is our blessed Lord who Himself brings believing sinners into the presence of God, who presents and introduces them. The word was used in classical Greek especially of access to a king's presence. The French word *entree* is an excellent translation of *prosagoge*. Our Lord brings believers by virtue of His precious blood, not only into the presence of God the Father, but into His unlimited favor and His infinite grace. The verb *prosago* is used in I Peter 3:18 in the expression, "that He might bring us to God." The translation could read, "that He might provide for you an *entree* into the presence of God." The second, not the first person is found in the best texts.

COMFORT. There are three Greek words translated by the one word "comfort."

The first is *paregoria,* used only in Col. 4:11. The word in its verb form means "to address, exhort, to console, comfort, appease, soothe." There is a medicine called *Paregoric* which is given to infants as a sedative. It tends to soothe and quiet them. The manufacturers certainly chose the right Greek word to describe the medicinal effects of their product. How precious to think that while Paul was in prison, deprived of his liberty to preach, his fellow-workers by their activities in preaching the gospel, were a soothing, quieting influence to him. In that sense they were a comfort to him. The noun form means "comfort, solace, relief, alleviation, consolation." We Christians, filled with the Holy Spirit, can be all that to our sorely-tried fellow-saints. The word is found in a pagan letter of consolation on the occasion of a death.

The second word is *paramutheomai,* and is used in *John* 11:19, 31; *I Cor.* 14:13; *Phil.* 2:1; *I Thes.* 2:11, 5:14. The word means "to speak to or address one whether by way of admoni-

---

28. *Moulton and Milligan.*

tion and incentive, or to calm and console, hence to encourage, console."

The third word is *tharseo*. It is translated "Be of good cheer," or "Be of good comfort" in *Mt.* 9:2, 22, 14:27; *Mk.* 6:50, 10:49; *Lk.* 8:48; *John* 16:33; *Acts* 23:11. It means "be of good courage, be of good cheer." A related verb *tharreo* means "to be of good courage, to be hopeful, confident, to be bold." *Tharseo* is found in the papyri in the sentence "eye ... of my soul, take courage."[29]

The fourth word is *parakaleo*. The word is made up of the verb *kaleo,* which means "to call," and the preposition *para* which means "beside." Hence the compound word means "to call alongside." In classical Greek writers it meant "to call to one's side, call for, summon," the context indicating the purpose of the summons. It meant also "to address, speak to, (call to, call on)," which may be done in the way of ex- hortation, entreaty, comfort, instruction. Hence, there re- sults a variety of senses in which it is used. Then it came to mean "to beg, entreat, beseech." Finally, it comes to mean "to encourage, strengthen, to comfort." It combines the ideas of exhorting, comforting, and encouraging in Rom. 12:8; I Cor. 14:31; I Thes. 3:2. Moulton and Milligan in reporting this word in the papyri, do not list any place where it means "to comfort." Its chief meaning in the papyri was "to ask, beseech." It meant "please, I exhort, I urge." This is the way it is most frequently used in the N.T. It is translated by the word "comfort" in the following places: *Mt.* 2:18, 5:4; *Lk.* 16:25; *Acts* 16:40, 20:12; *I Cor.* 14:31; *II Cor.* 1:4, 6, 2:7, 7:6, 7, 13, 13:11; *Eph.* 6:22; *Col.* 2:2, 4:8; *I Thes.* 3:2, 7, 4:18, 5:11; *II Thes.* 2:17. *Parakaleo* is the word used most fre- quently to bring the idea of comfort. From its other uses, one can see that it is probably the strongest word of the four.

29. *Moulton and Milligan.*

COMFORTER. This word is the translation of *parakletos* which comes from the above word *parakaleo*. It is found in John 14:16, 26, 15:26, 16:7, where it is translated "comforter," and in I John 2:1, where it is rendered by the word "advocate." The verb *parakaleo* refers to the act of calling someone to one's side in order to help one. The noun *parakletos* refers to the one who is called upon to render aid. It was used in the law courts of one who pleads another's cause before a judge, a counsel for the defence, an advocate. In the widest sense it means "a helper, a succorer, one who aids another." In the three passages in the Gospel noted above, the Holy Spirit is the Comforter to the saint, not that He comforts him in the sense of consoling him merely, but that He is sent to be the One to come to the aid of the Christian in the sense of ministering to him in his spiritual life. In the first epistle of John (2:1), the Lord Jesus is the *parakletos* of the believer in the sense that He pleads our cause before our heavenly Father in relation to sin in the life of the Christian, praying us back into fellowship with God by the way of our confession and the cleansing blood.

TRANCE. This is the translation of the Greek word *ekstasis*. This word comes from the verb *existemi*. The simple verb *histemi* means "to stand," the prefixed preposition, "out," thus, the compound word means "to stand out." The noun *ekstasis* thus means "a standing out." A person in a trance is one who in a sense is standing out of himself. He is actually in his physical body, but his attention has been so engaged by something or someone else that his mind does not register the impressions given him by his senses. He might as well be out of his body so far as recognized sense sensations are concerned.

In the Greek classics, the word meant "any casting down of a thing from its proper place or state: a displacement, a throwing of the mind out of its normal state, an alienation of mind, whether such an alienation as will cause lunacy; or it may be that of a man who by some sudden emotion is transported as it were out of himself, so that in his rapt condition, although he is awake, his mind is so drawn off from all surrounding objects and wholly fixed on things divine that he sees and hears nothing but the forms and images lying within, and thinks that he perceives with his bodily eyes and ears realities shown him by God."[30] The word also meant "amazement," namely, the state of one who, either owing to the importance or the novelty of an event, is thrown into a state of blended fear and wonder. Our word "ecstacy" is derived from the Greek *ekstasis*.

The word is used in Acts 10:10, 11:5, where Peter was on the housetop. Literally, "a trance fell upon him." In order that the apostle might see that it was right for him to go to the home of Cornelius, God had to give him a vision. But in order for Peter to see the vision, God needed to have his entire attention. This was accomplished by the Holy Spirit so controlling his thinking, that his senses did not register their impressions upon his mind. A like thing happened to John on the island of Patmos (Rev. 1:10) where the Greek reads, "I became in the Spirit." That is, the Spirit-filled apostle entered into a state in which the absolute control of the Spirit obtained. This was for the purpose of giving John the visions in the Book of the Revelation. Paul experienced a like thing while he was in the Temple (Acts 22:17, 18). The Lord Jesus appeared to Paul in order to give him a most important command.

These three recorded instances of Spirit-wrought trances occurred before the revelation was closed. Such trances are not now in order, for the Holy Spirit works through the written word of God.

In Mk. 5:42, the word is used in its verb and noun form in the words, "They were astonished with a great astonish-

---

30. *Thayer, Greek English Lexicon.*

ment." This was the effect of the bringing back to life of the daughter of the ruler of the synagogue. One could render it, "They were beside themselves with great amazement." Such was the effect of the miracle upon those who saw it that their senses were not registering. All they could think about, to the exclusion of everything else, was the miracle. The word is used in Mk. 16:8. Such was the effect upon those who saw the empty sepulchre, that they were beside themselves with amazement. In Lk. 5:26 the healing of the paralytic produced a like result.

The verb *existemi* is found in the following places and is translated by the words "were amazed, is beside himself, were astonished, bewitched, wondered;" *Mt.* 12:23; *Mk.* 2:12, 3:21, 5:42, 6:51; *Lk.* 2:47, 8:56, 24:22; *Acts* 2:7, 12, 8:9, 11, 13, 9:21, 10:45, 12:16; *II Cor.* 5:13. One can see that the words "amazed, wondered, astonished" hold a larger content of meaning and are far stronger in their New Testament usage than in our ordinary conversation. In the case of Simon the sorcerer, the word carries more than the idea of causing profound amazement. It is that his power over the people of Samaria was such that they acted under his spell as people would do who were so controlled by someone else that their normal sense functions did not register. Simon stood them out of themselves, so to speak. As the Holy Spirit controlled Peter, John, and Paul with the result that they received visions, so the power of Satan controlled these Samaritans in their actions while they were under the spell of Simon.

IMPUTED, RECKONED, COUNTED, ACCOUNTED, are translations of the Greek word *logizomai*. The word in the classics meant "to count, reckon, calculate, compute, to set to one's account." We will study its use in Gal. 3:6 as an illustration of its use in other passages. The word is used in the papyri as a business term: for instance, *"put to one's account;* let my revenues be *placed on deposit* at the store-

house; *reckoning* the wine to him at 16 drachmae the mono-
chore; a single artabae *being reckoned* at 180 myriads of
denari; I now give orders generally with regard to all payments actually made or *credited* to the government."[31]

Thus Abraham believed God, and his act of faith was
placed to his account in value as righteousness. He believed
God and his act of faith was *placed on deposit for him and
evaluated* as righteousness. He believed God and his act of
faith was *computed as to its value, and there was placed to his
account,* righteousness. He believed God, and his act of faith
was credited to his account for righteousness. Finally, he believed God, and his act of faith *was credited to him,* resulting
in righteousness.

All this does not mean, however, that Abraham's act of
faith was looked upon as a meritorious action deserving of
reward. It was not viewed as a good work by God and rewarded by the bestowal of righteousness. That would be salvation by works. But the fact that Abraham cast off all dependence upon good works as a means of finding acceptance
with God, and accepted God's way of bestowing salvation, was
answered by God in giving him that salvation. *Abraham
simply put himself in the place where a righteous God could
offer him salvation upon the basis of justice satisfied, and in
pure grace. God therefore put righteousness to his account.
He evaluated Abraham's act of faith as that which made it
possible for Him to give him salvation.*

The word *logizomai* is translated "imputed" in Rom. 4:6,
8, 11, 22, 23, 24; II Cor. 5:19; Jas. 2:23. In Rom. 4:8, the man
is called blessed, to whose account no sin is charged. At the
Cross, his sin was charged to the account of the Lord Jesus.
In Rom. 4:6, the man to whose account righteousness is put,
is called blessed. This is imputation, the act of putting something to someone's account. In the case of the Lord Jesus,
the sin of the human race was charged to Him. In the case

31. *Moulton and Milligan.*

of the believing sinner, the righteousness of God, Christ
Jesus Himself, is put to his account.

It is translated "counted" or "accounted" in the following
scriptures; Rom. 2:26, 4:3, 5; Gal. 3:6. In Rom. 2:26 we
have, "Shall not his uncircumcision be put to his account for
circumcision?"

The scripture where "reckoned" is used is Rom. 4:9, 10.
In II Tim. 4:16 we have an excellent illustration of the use
of *logizomai* in the words, "I pray God that it may not be
laid to their charge." The above treatment of *logizomai* is
chiefly confined to its use in connection with the substitu-
tionary atonement for sin. There are other uses which are
not covered by the foregoing work.

TRUTH, TRUE. This is the translation of the Greek
words *aletheia* and *alethes*. The words are a compound made
up of *lanthano* which means "to escape notice, to be unknown,
unseen, hidden, concealed," and the Greek letter Alpha prefixed. When a Greek wants to make a word mean the opposite to what it originally meant, he prefixes the Greek letter
Alpha. For instance, *dikaios* means "righteous," *adikaios,*
"unrighteous." Thus, *lanthano* means "hidden, concealed,"
and *alanthano* means "unhidden, unconcealed." The Greek
idea of truth is therefore that which is unconcealed, unhidden, that which will bear scrutiny and investigation, that
which is open to the light of day.

Thayer defines *aletheia* the noun (truth) as follows; "veri-
ty, truth, what is true in any matter under consideration." In
reference to religion, the word denotes "what is true in things
appertaining to God and the duties of man." When used of
the body of truth in Christianity, it refers to the truth as
taught therein respecting God and the execution of His purposes through Christ, and respecting the duties of man,
opposed alike to the superstitions of the Gentiles, the in-
ventions of the Jews, and the corrupt opinions and precepts of

false teachers. It is used also of that candor of mind which is free from affectation, pretence, simulation, falsehood, deceit. It is also used of sincerity of mind and integrity of character, also of a mode of life in harmony with divine truth. The noun *aletheia* (truth), the verb *aletheuo* (to speak the truth), and the adjective *alethes* (true), are all translated in the N.T., by the words "truth" or "true." There is another word *alethinos* which is also translated by the word "true," but which has an added content of meaning that throws further light upon the places where it is used.

The word *alethinos*, used twenty two times in John's writings and only five times in the rest of the N.T., means, "that which has not only the name and semblance, but the real nature corresponding to the name." It is particularly used to express that which is all that it pretends to be, for instance, pure gold as opposed to adulterated metal. In every respect it corresponds to the idea signified by the name. It is real and true, genuine. It is opposed to that which is fictitious, counterfeit, imaginary, simulated, and pretended. It is what we mean by the expression, "All wool and a yard wide." It contrasts realities with semblances. It is opposed to that which is imperfect, defective, frail, uncertain. The differences between *alethes*, and the word *alethinos* are covered up in the A.V., since both are translated by the one word "true."

For instance, in John 3:33 and Rom. 3:4, God is the *alethes* God in that He cannot lie (Tit. 1:2) . He is the truth-speaking and the truth-loving God. But in I Thes. 1:9 and John 17:3, He is the *alethinos* God. He is not like idols and other false gods that are the product of the diseased fancy of man, but a God who in His completeness of Being has the real nature corresponding to the name. He is in His Being all that the term "God" implies. In every respect He corresponds to the idea which is signified by the term "God." In the words of the Nicene creed, the Lord Jesus is *very* God of *very* God. The Latin Vulgate distinguishes between the word *alethes* and *alethinos* by the use of *verax* for the former, and the word *verus* (very) for the latter. By the words "Very God of Very God" we mean therefore that the Lord Jesus is *alethinos* God. He is in His Being all that the term "God" implies. We have almost lost the word *verus* (very) as an adjective, retaining it only as an adverb. Thus the word "truth" must do duty for both words, with a consequent loss of part of the meaning of the second word. Wycliffe's translation of John 15:1 is, "I am the *verri* vine," that is, the *alethinos* vine, the vine that corresponds in all details to what one would expect of the Lord Jesus as a Vine. This does not deny that Israel also was God's vine (Ps. 80:8; Jer. 2:21). But it does imply that no vine except the Lord Jesus realized this name in the sense that He was all that the name implied, and that to the full.

Trench says that "it does not of necessity follow, that whatever may be contrasted with the *alethinos* must thereby be concluded to have no substantial existence, to be altogether false and fraudulent. Inferior and subordinate realizations, partial and imperfect anticipations of the truth, may be set over against the truth in its highest form, in its ripest and completest development; and then to this last alone the title *alethinos* will be vouchsafed."

The Lord Jesus is the *alethinos* light (John 1:9). But that does not deny that John the Baptist was also a "burning and a shining light" (John 5:35). It does mean that our Lord Jesus was in His glorious Person all that the term "light" demanded and implied, and that to the full, while John was not. Our Lord is the *alethinos* bread (John 6:32). This does not suggest that the bread which Moses gave Israel was not also "bread from heaven" (Ps. 105:40), but that the latter was bread in a secondary and inferior degree. It was not in the highest sense food, for it did not nourish man's spiritual nature. The word *alethinos* is found in the following places, and is translated by the word "true." *Lk.* 16:11; *John* 1:9, 4:23, 37, 6:32, 7:28, 15:1, 17:3, 19:35; *I Thes.* 1:9; *Heb.* 8:2,

9:24, 10:22; *I John* 2:8, 5:20; *Rev.* 3:7, 14, 6:10, 15:3, 16:7, 19:2, 9, 11, 21:5, 22:6. Make a study of these scriptures in the light of the additional meaning in the word *alethinos.* In all other places in the N.T., where the words "truth" or "true" occur, *aletheia, alethes* or *aletheuo* are found.

REGENERATION, RENEWING. These words have a vital relationship to one another, and so will be treated together. The word "regeneration" is found in Mt. 19:28 and Tit. 3:5, and is the translation of the Greek word *paliggenesia.* The word "renewing" is found in Rom. 12:2 and Tit. 3:5, and is the translation of *anakainosis.*

We will study the word *paliggenesia* first. Archbishop Trench says of this word; "*Paliggenesia* is one among the many words which the gospel found, and, so to speak, glorified; enlarged the borders of its meaning; lifted it up into a higher sphere; made it the expression of far deeper thoughts, of far mightier truths, than any of which it had been the vehicle before." He gives examples of its use before it was taken over into the New Testament where its content of meaning was enlarged. In some passages the word means revivification and only that. In the Pythagorean doctrine of the transmigration of souls, their reappearance in new bodies was called their *paliggenesia.* The Stoics used this word to speak of the periodic renovation of the earth in the springtime when it budded and blossomed again, awaking from its winter sleep, and in a sense, revived from its winter death. It was used of recollection or reminiscence which the Greeks carefully distinguished from memory. Memory, they said, is instinctive and is common to beasts and men. But recollection and reminiscence are more than merely remembering things. They are "the reviving of faded impressions by a distinct act of the will, the reflux, at the bidding of the mind, of knowledge that has once ebbed."[32] *Paliggenesia,* Trench says,

32. *Trench, Synonyms of the New Testament.*

"which has thus in heathen and Jewish Greek the meaning of a recovery, a restoration, a revival, yet never reaches, or even approaches, there the depth of meaning which it has acquired in Christian language."

The word *paliggenesia* is made up of the Greek word *palin* and *genesis*. *Palin* is an adverb meaning "back, again, back again." *Genesis* is a noun used in the N.T., in the sense of "origin, race, birth." It is rendered "birth" in Mt. 1:18. It means "race, lineage." It is translated "generation" in Mt. 1:1. It comes from the verb *ginomai* which means "to become, to begin to be." Used of persons it means "to become, to be born." In John 8:58 we have, "Before Abraham came into existence (i.e., was born), I am." "Was" is the A.V., translation of *ginomai* here, the verb which means "to come into existence." In Rom. 1:3, the words referring to our Lord, "which was made of the seed of David according to the flesh," could read, "who with reference to the flesh (His humanity), was born of the seed of David." Another clear case of the usage of *ginomai* in the sense of "to be born" is in Gal. 4:4 where the Greek reads "having become out of a woman as a source." The participle is aorist, the classification ingressive. The participle for *ginomai* refers here therefore to entrance into a new state. It was His humanity into which our Lord entered. This entrance into human existence had its source in a woman, the preposition being *ek* (*out of*) and the case being ablative, thus, ablative of source. This entrance into human existence was effected by the virgin birth. Thus, while *ginomai* means fundamentally "to become, to begin to be," it is used at times in the sense of "to begin to be by being born." The word *paliggenesia* therefore means "to be born again."

In John 3:3, reference is made by our Lord to regeneration, but there both the adverb and the verb are different. The verb is *gennao*, which in its active voice means "to beget," and in the passive voice, "to be born." The adverb is *anothen* which means either "from above," or, "again." The first meaning is ruled out in John 3:3 by two things in the context, the fact that Nicodemus understood our Lord to speak of a repetition of a birth, and the fact that our Lord designated the truth about the new birth as, not heavenly but earthly in its nature. The adverb *anothen* therefore in John 3:3 speaks of a second or repeated birth.

Now, *palin* and *anothen* are synonyms. Both words refer to the repetition of an act, but *anothen* includes in that act a reference to the beginning, and the idea of a going back to the starting-point. It means a repetition of the beginning, again from the outset on. When *anothen* is used, the emphasis is more upon the return to the very beginning. Regeneration consists of the impartation of the life of God, eternal life, to a sinner who is spiritually dead. This is, according to the meaning of *anothen*, not only a repetition of an act of giving spiritual life to an individual, but a repetition that goes back to the beginning or starting point. The new-birth is therefore, not a second birth to physical birth, but to the act of God imparting spiritual life to Adam as recorded in Gen. 2:7. The human race is thus conceived of here as having had the divine life of God as it stood in Adam, as having lost that divine life in Adam's fall, and as needing a second impartation of divine life through the *paliggenesia*, the new-birth.

In Tit. 3:5, *paliggenesia* (regeneration) is said to be one of the means God used in saving us. The preposition "by" is the translation of *dia*, the preposition of intermediate agency.

Regeneration is described as a washing here. The word is *lutron*, which word means "a bath." We have the same word used in Eph. 5:26 where the bath of water (genitive of description), the water-bath cleanses the life of the believer. The Word of God is conceived of as a water-bath cleansing the life by putting out of it things that are sinful, and introducing into it, things that are right. In our present text, regeneration is spoken of as a bath in that the impartation of the divine nature results in the cleansing of the life by the fact that the new life from God provides the believer with both the desire and power to do the will of God and to refuse to fulfil the behests of the evil nature whose power has been broken by the identification of the believer with the Lord Jesus in His death on the Cross.

The other instance of the use of *paliggenesia* is in Mt. 19:28. Here it is used of the new-birth of the entire creation which will occur after the Millennial Kingdom, when the curse now resting upon the material creation because of sin will be removed, and the universe will be restored to its pristine glory. This is spoken of in Rom. 8:21-22; II Peter 3:7-13; Rev. 21:1. Paul includes in this great event, the glorification of the saints which takes place 1000 years before at the Rapture of the Church, but which is followed by the glorification of those saints who will live and die after the Rapture, which ties the whole matter of glorification up with the final restoration of the universe.

Commenting on the use of *paliggenesia* for the regeneration of the individual sinner and also of the universe, Trench has the following to say: "Is then *paliggenesia* used in two different senses, with no common bond binding the diverse uses of it together? By no means: all laws of language are violated by any such supposition. The fact is, rather, that the word by our Lord is used in a wider, by the apostle in a narrower, meaning. They are two circles of meaning, one comprehending more than the other, but their center is the same. The *paliggenesia* which Scripture proclaims begins with the *mikrokosmos* (little world) of single souls; but it does not end with this; it does not cease its effectual working till it has embraced the whole *makrokosmos* (great world) of the universe. The primary seat of the *paliggenesia* is the soul of man; it is there, it extends in ever-widening circles; and, first, to his of this that St. Paul speaks; but, having established its center body; the day of resurrection being the day of *paliggenesia* for it."

Speaking of the use of *paliggenesia* in Mt. 19:28, Trench says: "Doubtless our Lord there implies, or presupposes, the resurrection, but He also includes much more. Beyond the day of resurrection, . . . a day will come when all nature shall put off its soiled work-day garments, and clothe itself in holy-day attire, 'the times of restitution of all things' (Acts 3:21); . . . a day by St. Paul regarded as one in the labor-pangs of which all creation is groaning and travailing until now (Rom. 8:21-23). Man is the present subject of the *paliggenesia,* and of the wondrous change which it implies; but in that day it will have included within its limits that whole world of which man is the central figure: and here is the reconciliation of the two passages, in one of which it is contemplated as pertaining to the single soul, in the other to the whole redeemed creation. These refer both to the same event, but at different epochs and stages of its development."

We come now to our other word, *anakainosis,* found only in the N.T., in Rom. 12:2 and Tit. 3:5, and translated in both places by the word "renewing." Commenting on the relationship of *paliggenesia* and *anakainosis* in Tit. 3:5, Trench has the following: "Our Collect for Christmas day expresses excellently well the relation in which the *paliggenesia* and the *anakainosis* stand to each other; we pray, 'that we being regenerate,' in other words, having been already made the subjects of the *paliggenesia,* 'may daily be renewed by the Holy Spirit,' may continually know the renewing of the Holy Spirit. In this Collect, uttering, as do so many, profound theological truth in forms at once the simplest and the most accurate, the new birth is contemplated as already past, as having found place once for all, while the 'renewal' or 'renovation' is daily proceeding, being as it is that gradual restoration of the divine image, which is ever going forward in him who, through the new birth, has come under the transforming powers of the world to come. It is called 'the renewal *of the Holy Ghost*' inasmuch as He is the efficient cause, by whom alone this putting on of the new man, and the putting off the old, is brought about.

"These two then are bound by the closest ties to one another; the second the following up, the consequence, the consummation of the first. The *paliggenesia* is that free act of God's mercy and power, whereby He causes the sinner to pass out of the kingdom of darkness into that of light, out of death into life; it is the 'born again' of John 3:3, the 'born of God' of I John 5:4, ... the 'born of incorruptible seed' of I Pet. 1: 23; in it that glorious word begins to be fulfilled, 'behold, I make all things new' (Rev. 21:5). In it,—not in the preparation for it, but in the act itself, — the subject of it is passive, even as the child has nothing to do with its own birth. With the *anakainosis* it is otherwise. This is the gradual conforming of the man more and more to that new spiritual world into which he has been introduced, and in which he now lives and moves; the restoration of the divine image; and in all this, so far from being passive, he must be a fellow-worker with God."

Rom. 12:2 in a fuller and expanded translation is as follows; "Stop perpetually assuming an outward expression which does not come from your inner being but is put on from the outside, an expression patterned after this age, but let your outward expression be changed, an outward expression which comes from your inner being, this changed outward expression being the result of the renewing of your mind, with a view to your putting to the test for the purpose of approving what is the will of God, that will which is good and well-pleasing and complete." Paul is exhorting the saints here to stop masquerading in the habiliments of the world, and instead to yield themselves to the ministry of the Holy Spirit who will gradually produce in them the mind of Christ. Thus, they will be giving outward expression of their true inner regenerated Spirit-filled beings. The act of regeneration made them partakers of the divine nature. This is the basis upon which the Holy Spirit works in the Christian's life. *He has in His hands now an individual who has both the desire and the power to do the will of God. He augments this by His control over the saint when that saint yields to Him and cooperates with Him.* The first is *paliggenesia,* the second, *anakainosis,* the first, regeneration, the second, renewing (Tit. 3:5).

SIN. There are nine different Greek words in the N.T., which present sin in its various aspects, *hamartia, hamartema, parakoe, anomia, paranomia, parabasis, paraptoma, agnoema,* and *hettema.*

The word used most frequently in the N.T., is *hamartia.* This word in classical Greek never approaches the depth of meaning it has in the Bible. The pagan Greeks used it of a warrior who hurls his spear and fails to strike his foe. It is used of one who misses his way. *Hamartia* is used of a poet who selects a subject which it is impossible to treat poetically, or who seeks to attain results which lie beyond the limits of his art. The *hamartia* is a fearful mistake. It sometimes is employed in an ethical sense where the ideas of right and wrong are discussed, but it does not have the full significance of the biblical content of the word. In the moral sphere, it had the idea of missing the right, of going wrong. In the classics, its predominating significance was that of the failure to attain in any field of endeavor. Brought over into the N.T., this idea of failing to attain an end, gives it the idea of missing the divinely appointed goal, a deviation from what is pleasing to God, doing what is opposed to God's will, perversion of what is upright, a misdeed. Thus the word *hamartia* means a missing of the goal conformable to and fixed by God. It is interesting to note that in Romans the word *dikaiosune* which means "conformity to the standard" appears as the opposite of *hamartia,* a missing of the standard set by God

(6:16-18). The noun *hamartia* is everywhere translated in the N.T., by the word "sin" except in II Cor. 11:7, where it is rendered "offence," since the context speaks of Paul's relations to the Corinthians. In Eph. 1:7, 2:5, Col. 2:13, the word "sins" is not *hamartia* but *paraptoma*. The verb of the same root is also translated by the word "sin" except in Mt. 18:15, Lk. 17:3, 4, (trespass); Acts 25:8 (offended), I Pet. 2:20 (for your faults, i.e., having sinned).

The second word is *hamartema*. This word differs from *hamartia* in that it "is never sin regarded as sinfulness, or as the act of sinning, but only sin contemplated in its separate outcomings and deeds of disobedience to a divine law."[33] It is found in Mk. 3:28, 4:12; Rom. 3:25; I Cor. 6:18.

The third word is *parakoe*. It means "a failing to hear, a hearing amiss," the idea of active disobedience which follows on this inattentive or careless hearing, being superinduced upon the word. The sin is regarded as already committed in the failing to listen when God is speaking. In the O.T., the act of refusing to listen to God is described as disobedience (Jer. 11:10, 35:17). In Acts 7:57 this is seen very clearly. *Parakoe* is found in Rom. 5:19; II Cor. 10:6, and Heb. 2:2, where it is translated by the word "disobedience" in each case. What a flood of light is thrown upon Adam's original sin. He was careless about listening to the commands of God, inattentive when God was speaking. Then followed the act of disobedience to the divine command. The lack of an earnest and honest attempt to know God's will in any instance, is sin. This carelessness or inattentiveness with respect to the will of God, has its roots in the desire to have one's own way, and to cover up that desire and the consequent wrongdoing by the excuse that one did not know His will in the particular instance.

The fourth word is *anomia*. The word is a compound of the word *nomos* (law) and the letter Alpha which makes the

33. *Trench.*

whole word mean literally "no law." The word means "contempt or violation of law, lawlessness." It refers to the condition or deed of one who is acting contrary to the law. It is set over against the Greek word *dikaiosune* (righteousness) in II Cor. 6:14. That is, "what things does righteousness have in common with *anomia* (lawlessness)?" The word *dikaiosune* refers to a fixed and objective standard of life set up by God. Any deviation from that standard is an act contrary to law. The word is used in classical Greek writings, joined with *anarchia*, which is defined as "the state of a people without government, without lawful government, lawlessness, anarchy." The word is made up of *archos*, "a leader, a chief, a commander" and Alpha, the compound word meaning "without a leader or commander." Thus, anyone in a regularly constituted government who does not recognize and obey that government is *anarchos*, without law, an anarchist, thus, *anomia*, lawless. The word is used in the N.T., of one who acts contrary to law. The word *paranomia* refers to the act of one going beyond the limits which the law lays down. It is used only in II Pet. 2:16. *Anomia* is found in the following places where it is translated either "iniquity" or "the transgression of the law." *Mt.* 7:23, 13:41, 23:28, 24:12; *Rom.* 4:7, 6:19, *II Cor.* 6:14; *II Thes.* 2:7; *Tit.* 2:14; *Heb.* 1:9, 8:12, 10:17; *I John* 3:4.

The next word is *parabasis.* It comes from *parabaino* which means "to step on one side" thus, "to transgress, violate." It is translated by the word "transgression" in the N.T., except in Rom. 2:23 where the A.V., has "breaking" the law. Trench says of this word; "There must be something to transgress before there can be a transgression. There was sin between Adam and Moses, as was attested by the fact that there was death; but those between the law given in Paradise (Gen. 2:16, 17) and the law given from Sinai, sinning indeed, yet did not sin 'after the similitude of Adam's transgression' (*parabaseos* Rom. 5:14). With the law came for the first time the possibility of the transgression of law (Rom. 4:15) ." This word is found in Rom. 2:23, 4:15, 5:14; Gal. 3:19; I Tim. 2:14; Heb. 2:2, 9:15.

Paraptoma is our next word. This word comes from *parapipto* which means "to fall beside" a person or thing. Thus *paraptoma* means "a fall beside, a lapse or deviation from truth and uprightness." Cremer defines the word as follows: "a fault, a mistake, an offence, neglect, error." He says that *"Paraptoma* does not in Scripture as in profane Greek, imply palliation or excuse, . . . it denotes sin as a missing and violation of right . . . It may therefore be regarded as synonymous with *parabasis,* which designates sin as a transgression of a known rule of life, and as involving guilt . . . Still the word is not quite as strong as *parabasis,* . . . See for instance Gal. 6:1 . . . where, though a sin involving guilt is clearly meant, a missing of the mark, rather than a transgression of the law, is the form of sin referred to. We must accordingly affirm that *parabasis* denotes *sin objectively viewed,* as a violation of a known rule of life, but that in *paraptoma* reference is specially made to the subjective passivity and suffering of him who misses or falls short of the enjoined command; and the word has come to be used both of great and serious guilt, . . . and generally of all sin, even though unknown and unintentional (Ps. 19:13, Gal. 6:1) , so far as this is simply a missing of the right, and involves but little guilt, therefore a *missing* or *failure* including the activity and passivity of the acting subject." In Gal. 6:1 we have the case of Christians who, having been the subjects of the ministry of the Holy Spirit, had in following the teaching of the Judaizers, put themselves thereby under law, and thus had deprived themselves of the victory over sin which the Spirit had been giving them. They were trying their best in their own strength to live a life of victory over sin, and sin had taken them unawares. Sin had entered their experience before they knew it, for they were shorn of the victorious power which they previously had had. This is *paraptoma,* a sin which was not on their part a conscious disobedience of the will of God, but an unintentional one committed through the inability to prevent it entering the life. The word is found in the following places where it is translated "trespass, offence, fall, fault;" *Mt.* 6:14, 15, 18:35; *Mk.* 11:25, 26; *Rom.* 4:25, 5:15, 16, 17, 18, 20, 11:11, 12; *II Cor.* 5:19; *Gal.* 6:1; *Eph.* 1:7, 2:1, 5; *Col.* 2:13; *Jas.* 5:16.

The next word is *agnoema.* This word comes from *agnoeo,* a verb meaning "to be ignorant, not to understand, to sin through ignorance." Trench says of this word, "Sin is designated as an *agnoema* when it is desired to make excuses for it, so far as there is room for such, to regard it in the mildest possible light (see Acts 3:17). There is always an element of ignorance in every human transgression, which constitutes it human and not devilish; and which, while it does not take away, yet so far mitigates the sinfulness of it, as to render its forgiveness not indeed necessary, but possible. Thus compare the words of the Lord, 'Father, forgive them, for they know not what they do' (Lk. 23:34), with those of St. Paul, 'I obtained mercy because I did it ignorantly, in unbelief' (I Tim. 1:13)." Commenting on the usage of this word in Heb. 10:26, the only place where it is used in the N.T., Trench says, "There is therefore an eminent fitness in the employment of the word on the one occasion referred to already, where it appears in the N.T. The *agnoemata,* or 'errors' of the people, for which the High Priest offered sacrifice on the great day of atonement, were not wilful transgressions, 'presumptuous sins' (Ps. 19:13), committed against . . . conscience and with a high hand against God; those who committed such were cut off from the congregation; no provision having been made in the Levitical constitution for the forgiveness of such (Num. 15:30, 31), but they were sins growing out of the weakness of the flesh, out of an imperfect insight into God's law, out of heedlessness and lack of due circumspection (. . .

Lev. 4:13; compare 5:15-19; Num. 15:22-29), and afterwards looked back on with shame and regret."

Our last word is *hettema*. This word does not appear in classical Greek. A briefer form of the word, *hetta* is used, and is opposed to *nika* (victory). It means " a discomfiture, a worsting to victory." It is used twice in the N.T., in Rom. 11:12 where it has the non-ethical sense of diminution, decrease, and in I Cor. 6:7 where it has the ethical sense of coming short of duty, a fault.

To summarize: Sin in the N.T., is regarded as the missing of a mark or aim (*hamartia* or *hamartema*); the overpassing or transgressing of a line (*parabasis*); the inattentiveness or disobedience to a voice (*parakoe*); the falling alongside where one should have stood upright (*paraptoma*); the doing through ignorance of something wrong which one should have known about (*agnoema*); the coming short of one's duty (*hettema*); and the non-observance of a law (*anomia*).

HUMILITY, MEEKNESS, GENTLENESS. We will treat these words together, for they are closely related to one another.

The word "humility" is the translation of *tapeinophrosune* which hereafter in this study will be designated by the abbreviation *tap.*, because of its length. Trench says of this word: "The work for which Christ's gospel came into the world was no less than to put down the mighty from their seat, and to exalt the humble and meek. It was then only in accordance with this its mission that it should dethrone the heathen virtue *megalopsuchia* (human magnanimity and great souledness), and set up the despised Christian grace *tap.*, in its room, stripping that of the honor it had unjustly assumed, delivering this from the dishonor which as unjustly had clung to it hitherto; and in this direction advancing so far that a Christian writer has called this last not merely a grace, but the casket or treasure house in which all other graces are contained . . . And indeed not the grace only, but the very word *tap.*, is itself a fruit of the gospel; no Greek writer employed it before the Christian era, nor, apart from the influence of Christian writers, after."

The word usually used by pagan writers which is related to *tap.*, the New Testament word, was *tapeinos*. Speaking of the use of the latter by the Greek writers, Trench says: "The instances are few and exceptional in which *tapeinos* signifies anything for them which is not grovelling, slavish, and mean-spirited." He states that this word is associated in the Greek classics with such words as the following: *aneleutheros* (not free, illiberal, slavish, servile, niggardly, stingy), *agennes* (without illustrious birth, low-born, cowardly, mean), *katephes* (downcast). But he also shows that at times the word was used with a better meaning. It is linked by Plato with a word that speaks of certain ones who were honored. Demosthenes uses it to describe words that are also moderate, modest, and temperate. Xenophon sets it over against those who are described as holding themselves to be above others. Plutarch says that the purpose of divine punishment is that the soul may become wise, prudent (*tapeinos*), and fearful before the face of God. Following these latter examples of the good use of the word *tapeinos* in pagan literature, Trench has this to say: "Combined with these prophetic intimations of the honor which should one day be rendered even to the very words expressive of humility, it is very interesting to note that Aristotle himself has a vindication, and it only needs to receive its due extension to be a complete one, of the Christian *tap.* . . .

"Having confessed how hard it is for a man to be truly great-souled, for he will not allow any great-souledness which does not rest on corresponding realities of goodness and moral greatness, . . . he goes on to observe, though merely by the way and little conscious how far his words reach, that to think humbly of one's self, *where that humble estimate is the true one,* cannot be imputed to any culpable meanness of spirit: it is rather the true *sophrosune* (good sense, prudence, sobriety, sensibleness). But if this be so (and who will deny it?), then, seeing that for every man the humble estimate of himself is the true one, Aristotle has herein unconsciously vindicated *tap.,* as a grace in which every man ought to abound; for that which he, even according to the standard which he set up, confessed to be a *chalepon* (a difficult thing), namely to be truly great-souled, the Christian, convinced by the Spirit of God, and having in his Lord a standard of perfect righteousness before his eyes, knows to be not merely a *chalepon,* but an *adunaton* (an impossibility). Such is the Christian *tap.,* no mere modesty or absence of pretension, which is all that the heathen would at the very best have found in it; nor yet a selfmade grace; and Chrysostom is in fact bringing in pride again under the disguise of humility, when he characterizes it as a making of ourselves small, *when we are great* . . . Far truer and deeper is St. Bernard's definition: 'the esteeming of ourselves small, inasmuch as we are so; the thinking truly, and because truly, therefore lowlily, of ourselves'.

"But it may be objected, how does this account of Christian *tap.,* as springing out of and resting on the sense of unworthiness, agree with the fact that the sinless Lord laid claim to this grace, and said, 'I am meek and lowly in heart' (*tapeinos,* . . . Mt. 11:29)? The answer is, that for the sinner *tap.,* involves the confession of sin, inasmuch as it involves the confession of his true condition; while yet for the unfallen creature the grace itself as truly exists, involving for such the acknowledgement not of *sinfulness,* which would be untrue, but of *creatureliness,* of absolute dependence, of having nothing, but receiving all things of God. And thus the grace of humility belongs to the highest angel before the throne, being as he is a creature, yea, even to the Lord of Glory Himself. In His human nature He must be the pattern of all humility, of all creaturely dependence; and it is only *as a man* that Christ thus claims to be *tapeinos*: His human life was a constant living on the fulness of His Father's love; He evermore, as man, took the place which beseemed the creature in the presence of its Creator."

Cremer has a helpful note on *tapeinos*. "The word is used in profane Greek very often in a morally contemptible sense, namely, cringing, servile, low, common, . . . and it is a notable peculiarity of Scripture usage that the LXX., Apocrypha and N.T., know nothing of this import of the word, but rather, in connection with, deepen the conception, and raise the word to be the designation of the noblest and most necessary of all virtues, which in contrast with *hubris* (wanton violence arising from the pride of strength, insolence) in every form is still something quite different from the *sophrosune* (good sense, prudence, sobriety, sensibleness) which is opposed to *hubris* among the Greeks. It is the disposition of the man who esteems himself as small before God and men, takes a low estimate of himself, . . . a representation foreign to profane Greek, though a presentiment of this virtue is traceable there." Cremer says that the Greek expression for humility is found in the words *poiein ta dikaia sigei*. That translated would be, "to habitually do the just and righteous things in a quiet way unnoticed by others." Then he adds, "But it must not be overlooked that this subdued stillness of feeling was no more than *a part* of humility, and the expression by no means attained or sufficed for the biblical conception, especially as denoting humility manifested before God, which arises from the perception of sin, or is at least inseparably connected therewith (. . . Luke 18:14); of this the Greeks had no presentiment. Humility with the Greeks was in fact nothing higher than *modesty, unassuming diffidence.* . . . The Greek *tapeinos* is nothing more than an element of *sophrosune* (good sense, prudence, sobriety, sensibleness), and in direct contrast with the *tap.*, of Scripture, it is in no way opposed to self-righteousness. But the other element in humility, Phil. 2:3, "In lowliness of mind (*tap.*) let each esteem other better than themselves," is opposed to the Greek conception of *dikaiosune* (justice), which, while not self-seeking, is not the least unselfish, but gives to everyone his own. Hence it is clear why we find in the N.T., as a substantial designation of humility, a new word, *tapeinophrosune.*"

We have dwelt at considerable length upon the classical use of the N.T., words which mean *humility,* in order to more clearly define the content of meaning in the Christian use of these words. We have used the classical usage as a dark background against which the N.T., usage shines more clearly. We can well understand why the Greeks had no proper conception of humility. True humility is a product of the Holy Spirit in the yielded believer. The only self-description that ever fell from our Lord's lips was, "I am meek and lowly" (*tapeinos* Mt. 11:29). Paul singles out this grace of humility (*tap.*) as the keynote that explains the mind of Christ (Phil. 2:3). Peter speaks of humility (*tap.*) as that particular virtue which makes all the other Christian graces what they should be (I Pet. 5:5).

Thayer gives the following definition of *tap*: "the having a humble opinion of one's self; a deep sense of one's (moral) littleness; modesty, humility, lowliness of mind." For *tapeinos* Thayer gives: "not rising far from the ground, lowly, of low degree, lowly in spirit, humble."

The word *tapeinophrosune* occurs in Acts 20:19; Eph. 4:2; Phil. 2:3; Col. 2:18, 23, 3:12; I Pet. 5:5, and is translated in these places by the words "humility, lowliness of mind, humbleness of mind." In Col. 2:18, 23, it is used of the affected and ostentatious humility of the Gnostics. The word *tapeinos* is found in *Mt.* 11:29; *Lk.* 1:52; *Rom.* 12:16; *II Cor.* 7:6, 10:1; *Jas.* 1:9, 4:6; *I Pet.* 5:5. It is translated "lowly, low degree, low estate, cast down, base, humble." *Tapeinosis,* a word of the same stem, occurs in *Lk.* 1:48; *Acts* 8:33, *Phil.*

3:21; *Jas.* 1:10, where it is translated "low estate, humiliation, vile, made low." This word means "lowness, low estate," and is used metaphorically in the sense of spiritual abasement which leads one to perceive and lament his moral littleness and guilt, as in Jas. 1:10. The verb *tapeinoo* is found in *Mt.* 18:4, 23:12; *Lk.* 3:5, 14:11, 18:14; *II Cor.* 11:7, 12:21; *Phil.* 2:8, 4:12; *Jas.* 4:10; *I Pet.* 5:6. It means "to make low, bring low, to bring into a humble condition, to abase, to assign a lower rank or place to, to humble or abase one's self, to be ranked below others who are honored or rewarded, to have a modest opinion of one's self, to behave in an unassuming manner."

MEEKNESS. This word is the translation of *praotes.* Trench says of this Greek word: "The gospel of Christ did not rehabilitate *praotes* so entirely as it had done *tapeinophrosune,* but this, because the word did not need rehabilitation to the same extent. *Praotes* did not require to be transformed from a bad sense to a good, but only to be lifted up from a lower level of good to a higher. This indeed it did need; for no one can read Aristotle's portraiture of the *praos* and of *praotes* . . ., mentally comparing the heathen virtue with the Christian grace, and not feel that Revelation has given these words a depth, a richness, a fulness of significance which they were very far from possessing before. The great moralist of Greece set *praotes* as the *mesotes peri orges* (a mean or middle, a state between two extremes), between the two extremes, *orgilotes* (irascibility, the nature of a person who is easily provoked or inflamed to anger), and *aorgesia* (defective in the passion of anger, the nature of a person who lacks gall), with, however, so much leaning to the latter that it might very easily run into this defect; and he finds it worthy of praise, more because by it a man retains his own equanimity and composure, . . . than for any nobler reason. Neither does Plutarch's own graceful little essay, *"Peri*

Aorgesias" (Concerning Lack of Gall), rise anywhere to a loftier pitch than this, though we might have looked for something higher from him. *Praotes* is opposed by Plato to *agriotes* (fierceness, cruelty) . . .; by Aristotle to *chalepotes* (roughness, ruggedness, harshness) . . .; by Plutarch or some other under his name, to *apotomia* (severity) . . .; all indications of a somewhat superficial meaning by them attached to the word.

"Those modern expositors who will not allow for the new forces at work in sacred Greek, who would fain restrict, for instance, the *praotes* of the N.T., to that sense which the word, as employed by the best classical writers, would have borne, deprive themselves and as many as accept their interpretation, of much of the deeper teaching in Scripture. . . . The scriptural *praotes* is not in a man's outward behavior only; nor yet in his relations to his fellow-men; as little in his mere natural disposition. Rather is it an inwrought grace of the soul; and the exercises of it are first and chiefly towards God (Mt. 11: 29; Jas. 1:21). It is that temper of spirit in which we accept His dealings with us as good, and therefore without disputing or resisting; and it is closely linked with *tapeinophrosune,* and follows directly upon it (Eph. 4:2; Col. 3:12; compare Zeph. 3:12); because it is only the humble heart which is also the meek; and which, as such, does not fight against God, and more or less struggle and contend with Him.

"This meekness, however, being first of all a meekness before God, is also such in the face of men, even of evil men, out of a sense that these, with the insults and injuries which they may inflict, are permitted and employed by Him for the chastening and purifying of His elect. This was the root of David's *praotes,* when Shimei cursed and flung stones at him— the consideration, namely, that the Lord had bidden him (II Sam. 16:11), that it was just for him to suffer these things, however unjustly the other might inflict them; and out of like convictions all true Christian *praotes* must spring. He that is meek indeed will know himself a sinner among sinners; — or, if there was One who could not know Himself such, yet He too bore the sinner's doom, and endured the contradiction of sinners (Lk. 9:35, 36; John 18:22, 23); and this knowledge of his own sin will teach him to endure meekly the provocations with which they may provoke him, and not to withdraw himself from the burdens which their sin may impose upon him (Gal. 6:1; II Tim. 2:25; Tit. 3:2).

"*Praotes,* then, or meekness, if more than mere gentleness of manner, if indeed the Christian grace of meekness of spirit, must rest on deeper foundations than its own, on those namely which *tapeinophrosune* has laid for it, and can only subsist while it continues to rest on these. It is a grace in advance of *tapeinophrosune,* not as more precious than it, but as presupposing it, and as being unable to exist without it."

Praotes is found in *I Cor.* 4:21; *II Cor.* 10:1; *Gal.* 5:23, 6:1; *Eph.* 4:2; *Col.* 3:12; *I Tim.* 6:11; *II Tim.* 2:25; *Tit.* 3:2. The adjective *praos* (meek) occurs in Mt. 11:29.

GENTLENESS. This is the translation of *epieikeia.* Trench has the following to say regarding this word: "*Tapeinophrosune* (humility) and e*pieikeia* (gentleness), though joined together by Clement of Rome . . ., are in their meanings too far apart to be fit subjects of synonymous discrimination; but *praotes* (meekness), which stands between, holds on to both. The attempt has just been made to seize its points of contact with *tapeinophrosune.* Without going over this ground anew, we may consider the relations to *epieikeia* in which it stands.

"The mere existence of such a word as *epieikeia* is itself a signal evidence of the high development of ethics among the Greeks. It expresses exactly that moderation which recognizes the impossibility cleaving to all formal law, of anticipating and providing for all cases that will emerge, and present themselves to it for decision; which, with this, recognizes the danger that ever waits upon the assertion of *legal* rights, lest they should be pushed into *moral* wrongs; . . . which, therefore, urges not its own rights to the uttermost, but, going back in part or in the whole from these, rectifies and redresses the unjustices of justice. It is thus more truly just than strict justice would have been . . . . He (Aristotle) sets the *akribodikaios* (severely judging, extreme to mark what is amiss), the man who stands up for the last tittle of his legal rights, over against the *epieikes*. . . . This aspect of *epieikeia*, namely, that it is a going back from the letter of right for the better preserving of the spirit, must never be lost sight of . . . .

"The archetype and pattern of this grace is found in God. All His goings back from the strictness of His rights as against men; all His allowance of their imperfect righteousness, and giving of a value to that which, rigorously estimated, would have none; all His refusals to exact extreme penalties; . . . all His keeping in mind whereof we are made, and measuring His dealings with us thereby; all of these we may contemplate as *epieikeia* upon His part; even as they demand in return the same, one toward another, upon ours. Peter, when himself restored, must strengthen his brethren (Lk. 22:32). The greatly forgiven servant in the parable (Mt. 18:23), having known the *epieikeia* of his lord and king, is justly expected to show the same to his fellow servant. The word is often joined with *philanthropia* (friendliness, humanity, benevolence, liberal conduct, liberality); . . . with *hemerotes* (gentleness, kindness); . . . with *makrothumia* (longsuffering, forbearance); with *anexikakia* (forbearance); . . . often too with *praotes*."

The word *epieikeia* is defined by Thayer as follows: "mildness, gentleness, fairness, sweet reasonableness." It occurs in Acts 24:4 and II Cor. 10:1. *Epieikes*, a word of the same root, is defined by the same authority as follows: "seemly, suitable, equitable, fair, mild, gentle." It is found in *Phil.* 4:5; *I Tim.* 3:3; *Tit.* 3:2; *Jas.* 3:17; *I Pet.* 2:18.

We now offer a brief summary of the treatment of the three words "humility," "meekness," and "gentleness," pointing out their meanings and the distinctions that exist between them.

Humility is not mere modesty or absence of pretension, nor is it a self-made grace such as making ourselves small when we are great, but it is the esteeming of ourselves small, inasmuch as we are so, the thinking truly, and because truly, therefore lowlily of ourselves.

Meekness is that temper of spirit in which we accept God's dealings with us as good, without disputing or resisting them. The meek man will not fight against God, and more or less struggle or contend with Him. Meekness is also shown towards our fellow-man who mistreats us, insults us, treats us with injustice, in that the one who is being injured endures patiently and without any spirit of retaliation the provocations that are imposed upon him. The meek man will not withdraw himself from the burdens which other men's sins may impose upon him.

Gentleness is that temper of spirit which expresses exactly that moderation which recognizes the impossibility cleaving to all formal law, of anticipating and providing for all cases that will emerge and present themselves for decision; which with this, recognizes the danger that ever waits upon the assertion of legal rights, lest they should be pushed into moral wrongs, which therefore urges not its own rights to the uttermost, but, going back in part or in the whole from these, rectifies and redresses the unjustices of justice. Gentleness exhibits itself in the act of treating others with mildness, fairness, and sweet reasonableness.

Humility has to do with one's estimate of one's self, *meekness* with one's attitude toward the dealings of God and man with respect to one's self, and *gentleness* with one's treatment of others.

ENVY. This is the translation of two Greek words, *zelos*
and *phthonos*. Trench has the following to say about them:
"These words are often joined together; they are so by St.
Paul (Gal. 5:20, 21) (emulations *zelos*, envy *phthonos*); by
Clement of Rome . . ., by Cyprian, . . . by classical writers as
well, . . . and by others. Still, there are differences between
them; and this first, that *zelos* is . . . used sometimes in a good
(as John 2:17; Rom. 10:2; II Cor. 9:2), sometimes, and in
Scripture oftener, in an evil sense (as Acts 5:17; Rom. 13:13;
Gal. 5:20; Jas. 3:14), in which last place, to make quite clear
what *zelos* is meant, it is qualified by the addition of *pikros*
(bitter, harsh, virulent), and is linked with *eritheia* (a parti-
san and factious spirit which does not disdain low acts);
while *phthonos*, incapable of good, is used always and only
in an evil signification. When *zelos* is taken in good part, it
signifies the honorable emulation, with the consequent imitation, of that which presents itself to the mind's eye as excellent. . . . South here, as always, expresses himself well: 'We
ought by all means to note the difference between envy and
emulation; which latter is a brave and a noble thing, and
quite of another nature, as consisting only in a generous imitation of something excellent; and that such an imitation as
scorns to fall short of its copy, but strives, if possible, to outdo
it. The emulator is impatient of a superior, not by depressing
or maligning another, but by perfecting himself, so that while
that sottish thing envy sometimes fills the whole soul, as a
great dull fog does the air; this, on the contrary, inspires it
with new life and vigor, whets and stirs up all the powers of
it to action. And surely that which does so (if we also abstract it from those heats and sharpnesses that sometimes by
accident may attend it), must needs be in the same degree
lawful and laudable too, that it is for a man to make himself
as useful and accomplished as he can.' . . .

"By Aristotle *zelos* is employed exclusively in this nobler
sense, as that active emulation which grieves, not that another

has the good, but that itself has it not; and which, not pausing here, seeks to supply the deficiencies which it finds in itself. From this point of view he contrasts it with envy . . . Compare the words of our English poet: *'Envy, to which the ignoble mind's a slave, is emulation in the learned and the brave.'*

"But it is only too easy for this zeal and honorable rivalry to degenerate into a meaner passion; . . . those who *together* aim at the same object, who are thus competitors, being in danger of being enemies as well; . . . These degeneracies which wait so near upon emulation, and which sometimes cause the word itself to be used for that into which it degenerates ('pale and bloodless *emulation,*' Shakespeare), may assume two shapes: either that of the desire to make war upon the good which it beholds in another, and thus to trouble that good, and make it less; therefore we find *zelos* and *eris* (contention, strife, wrangling) continually joined together (Rom. 13:13; II Cor. 12:20; Gal. 5:20 . . .) . . . Where there is not vigor and energy enough to attempt the *making* of it less, there may be at least the *wishing* of it less; with such petty carping and fault-finding as it may dare to indulge in . . . *Phthonos* is the meaner sin, . . . being merely displeasure at another's good; . . . with the desire that this good or this felicity may be less; and this, quite apart from any hope that thereby its own will be more . . .; so that it is no wonder that Solomon long ago could describe it as 'the rottenness of the bones' (Prov. 14:30). He that is conscious of it is conscious of no impulse or longing to raise himself to the level of him whom he envies, but only to depress the envied to his own."

To summarize: *Zelos* in its good sense refers to that honorable emulation, with the consequent imitation, of that which presents itself to the mind's eye as excellent, an emulation which consists only in a generous imitation of something excellent, an imitation that scorns to fall short of its copy, but strives, if possible, to outdo it, the emulator being impatient of a superior, not by depressing or maligning another, but by perfecting himself, which inspires him with new life and vigor, and whets and stirs up all the powers of his being to action. Thayer gives the following meanings: "excitement of mind, ardor, fervor of spirit, zeal, ardor in embracing, pursuing, defending anything." *Zelos* is used in a good sense in *John* 2:17; *Rom.* 10:2; *II Cor.* 7:7, 11, 9:2, 11:2; *Phil.* 3:6; *Col.* 4:13; *Heb.* 10:27. The word is translated "zeal, fervent mind, jealousy, indignation."

Zelos in its evil sense refers to envy, the desire to make war upon the good which it beholds in another, and thus to trouble that good and make it less; or, where there is not vigor and energy enough to attempt the *making* of it less, there may be at least the *wishing* of it less; with such petty carping and fault-finding as it may dare to indulge. The word is used in its evil sense in Acts 5:17, 13:45; Rom. 13:13; I Cor. 3:3 12:20; Gal. 5:20; Jas. 3:14, 16. It is translated "indignation, envy, emulations."

Phthonos is displeasure at another's good, with the desire that this good or this felicity may be less, and this, quite apart from any hope that thereby its own will be more. It is used in *Mt.* 27:18; *Mk.* 15:10; *Rom.* 1:29; *Gal.* 5:21; *Phil.* 1:15; *I Tim.* 6:4; *Tit.* 3:3; *Jas.* 4:5; *I Pet.* 2:1. In each of these cases it is used in an evil sense except in Jas. 4:5, where the Holy Spirit who has been caused to take up His permanent abode in us, has a passionate desire to the point of envy (phthonos). The Holy Spirit is passionately desirous of controlling the believer so that He can perform His office-work of causing the saint to grow in the Christian life, and He is envious of any control which the evil nature may exert over the believer. He is displeased with the evil nature and the success it may have in controlling him, and passionately desires that this felicity of the evil nature may be less, and this, quite apart from any felicity He Himself might enjoy in controlling the Christian. Here is a divine envy entirely apart from sin, manifesting a holy hatred of sin, caring nothing for its own interests, but only that sin be put out of the believer's life.

REST. This is the single translation of two Greek words which speak of *rest* from two different points of view. These must be distinguished if the Bible student is to arrive at a full-orbed and clear interpretation of the passages in which each appears. Trench has the following on these words: "Our Version renders both these words by 'rest'; *anapausis* at Mt. 11:29, 12:43; and *anesis* at II Cor. 2:13, 7:5; II Thes. 1:7. No one can object to this; while yet, on a closer scrutiny, we perceive that they repose on different points of view. *Anapausis*, from *anapauo*, implies the pause or cessation from labor (Rev. 4:8); it is the constant word in the Septuagint for the rest of the Sabbath; thus Ex. 16:23, 31:15, 35:2, and often. *Anesis*, from *aniemi*, implies the relaxing or letting down of chords or strings, which have before been strained or drawn tight, its exact and literal antithesis being *epitasis* (a stretching) . . . thus Plato . . . 'in the tightening (*epitasis*) and slackening (*anesis*) of the strings! . . .' Plato has the same opposition between *anesin* and *spoude* (haste, speed); . . . while Plutarch sets *anesis* over against *stenochoria* (narrowness of space, a confined space), as a dwelling at large, instead of in a narrow and straight room; and St. Paul over against *thlipsis* (a pressure, oppression, affliction) (II Cor. 8:13), not willing that there should be 'ease' (*anesis*) to other Churches, and 'affliction' (*thlipsis*), that is from an excessive contribution, to the Corinthian. Used figuratively, it expresses what we, employing the same image, call the relaxation of morals (thus Athenaeus, 14:13: *akolasia* (licentiousness, intemperance, any excess or extravagance) *kai* (and) *anesis*, setting it over against *sophrosune* (good sense, sobriety, prudence).

"It will at once be perceived how excellently chosen *echein anesin* ("let him have liberty") at Acts 24:23 is, to express what St. Luke has in hand to record. Felix, taking now a

more favorable view of Paul's case, commands the centurion
who had him in charge, to *relax* the strictness of his imprison-
ment, to keep him rather under honorable arrest than in
actual confinement; which partial *relaxation* of his bonds is
exactly what this phrase implies. . . .

"The distinction, then, is obvious. When our Lord promises *anapausis* to the weary and heavy laden who come to Him
(Mt. 11:18, 29), His promise is, that they shall cease from
their toils; shall no longer spend their labor for that which
satisfieth not. When St. Paul expresses his confidence that
the Thessalonians, troubled now, should yet find *anesia* in the
day of Christ (II Thes. 1:7), he anticipates for them, not so
much cessation from labor, as relaxation of the chords of
affliction, now so tightly drawn, strained and stretched to the
uttermost. It is true that this promise and that at the heart
are not two, but one; yet for all this they present the blessedness which Christ will impart to His own under different
aspects, and by help of different images; and each word has
its own fitness in the place where it is employed."

The noun *anapausis* is found in Mt. 11:29, 12:43; Lk. 11:24;
Rev. 4:8, 14:11. The verb *anapauo,* which is of the same root,
and which means, "to cause or permit one to cease from any
movement or labor in order to recover and collect his strength,
to give rest, refresh, to give one's self rest, to take rest," occurs
in *Mt.* 11:28, 26:45; *Mk.* 6:31, 14:41; *Lk.* 12:19; *I Cor.* 16:18;
II Cor. 7:13; *Phm.* 7, 20; *I Pet.* 4:14; *Rev.* 6:11, 14:13. There
are illustrations of the use of these words in the papyri. Moulton and Milligan report the use of *anapausis* in the case of a
man over 70 who pleads for "relief" (*anapausis*) from public
duties; also in the case of veterans who have been released
from military service for a five years' rest. They say that the
essential idea of this word is that of a respite or *temporary*
rest as a preparation for future toil. They report the use of
the verb *anapauo* as a technical term of agriculture where a
farmer rests his land by sowing light crops upon it.

The word *anesis* is found in Acts 24:23 (liberty) ; II Cor. 2:13, 7:5, 8:13; II Thes. 1:7.

CHASTENING, ADMONITION. These are the respective translations of *paideia* and *nouthesia*. Trench has the following to say about these two Greek words: "It is worth while to attempt a discrimination between these words, occurring as they do together at Eph. 6:14, and being often there either not distinguished at all, or distinguished erroneously.

"*Paideia* is one among the many words, into which revealed religion has put a deeper meaning than it knew of, till this took possession of it; the new wine by a wondrous process making new even the old vessel into which it was poured. For the Greek, *paideia* was simply 'education;' nor, in all the definitions of it which Plato gives, is there the slightest prophetic anticipation of the new force which it one day should obtain. But the deeper apprehension of those who learned that 'foolishness is bound in the heart' alike 'of a child' and of a man, while yet 'the rod of correction may drive it far from him' (Prov. 22:15), led them, in assuming the word, to bring into it a further thought. They felt and understood that all effectual instruction for the sinful children of men, includes and implies chastening, or, as we are accustomed to say, out of a sense of the same truth, 'correction.' There must be *epanorthosis* (a setting right, a correcting, a revisal, an improvement), or 'rectification' in it; which last word, occurring but once in the N.T., is there found in closest connection with *paideia* (II Tim. 3:16).

"Two definitions of *paideia* — the one by a great heathen philosopher, the other by a great Christian theologian, — may be profitably compared. This is Plato's: '*Paideia* is the drawing on and the leading towards the right word which has been spoken according to its usage' (author's translation). And this is that of Basil the Great: 'The *Paideia* is a certain help given to the soul, a painstaking, laborious oft repeated

clearing out of the blemishes that come from wickedness'
(author's translation)." It will be observed that the pagan
Greek usage of *paideia* was limited to the education of the
intellect, whereas when the word was taken over into the N.T.,
an additional content of meaning was poured into it, for in
its Christian usage it refers to the education of the moral and
spiritual part of the individual's life, and that, principally,
in the eradication of sins, faults, and weaknesses present in
the life.

Taking up the other word, *nouthesia*, Trench says;
"*Nouthesia* . . . is more successfully rendered, 'admonition';
. . . It is the training by word — by the word of encourage-
ment, when this is sufficient, but also by that of remonstrance,
of reproof, of blame, where these may be required; as set over
against the training by act and by discipline, which is *paideia*.
. . . The distinctive feature of *nouthesia* is the training by
word of mouth. . . .

"Relatively, then, and by comparison with *paideia,*
nouthesia is the milder term; while yet its association with
paideia teaches us that this too is a most needful element of
Christian education; that the *paideia* without it would be
very incomplete; even as, when years advance, and there is no
longer a child, but a young man, to deal with, it must give
place to, or rather be swallowed up in, the *nouthesia* altogether. And yet the *nouthesia* itself, where need is, will be
earnest and severe enough; it is much more than a feeble
Eli-remonstrance: 'Nay, my sons, for it is no good report that
I hear (I Sam. 2:24)'; indeed, of Eli it is expressly recorded
in respect of those sons *ouk enouthetei autous* (he did not
admonish them) (3:13)."

From Trench's discussion it is clear that the word *paideia,*
translated "chastening" in the N.T., does not mean punishment. Nor does it mean merely instruction. Nor does it have
for its primary purpose, growth in the Christian virtues. Its
primary purpose is to rid the life of sins, faults, and weak-

nesses by corrective measures which God in His providence either sends or allows to come into the life.

Paideia is found in Eph. 6:4 in connection with *nouthesia*. Trench says that it should be rendered by the word "discipline" rather than by "nurture." The word "nurture" implies growth whereas *paideia* speaks of corrective measures designed to eliminate those things in the life that hinder growth. The same thing holds true in the case of II Tim. 3:16 where the word is rendered "instruction." In Heb. 12:5, 7, 8, 11, *paideia* is uniformly translated "chastening" and "chastisement."

The verb *paideuo* which has the same root as *paideia,* has its classical usage of "to chastise in the sense of punish" in Lk. 23:16, 22, and "to instruct" in Acts 7:22, 22:3, but in the following scriptures it refers to the corrective discipline of God's providential dealings with the believer, the purpose of which is to eliminate from the life those things which hinder Christian growth; I Cor. 11:32; II Cor. 6:9; I Tim. 1:20 (may learn); Heb. 12:6, 7, 10; Rev. 3:19. In II Tim. 2:25 and Tit. 2:12, *paideuo* refers to the discipline which the Word of God itself affords.

The word *nouthesia* is found only in I Cor. 10:11; Eph. 6:4, and Tit. 3:10, where it is rendered "admonition."

SERVANT. There are five Greeks word used in the N. T., that speak of one who renders service, the translation of which is not however uniformly given by the use of the single word "servant." They are *doulos, therapon, diakonos, oiketes,* and *huperetes.*

Doulos is the most common word. It designated one who was born into his condition of slavery, one bound to his master as his slave, one who was in a permanent relationship to his master, which relationship could only be broken by death, one whose will was swallowed up in the will of his master, one who served his master even to the extent that he disregarded his own interests. This word was used in the first

century world as a designation of a class of slaves that represented a most abject, servile condition. It is the word taken
over into the N.T., to designate a sinner as a slave (Rom.
6:17). It is also used to speak of a believer as a bondslave of
the Lord Jesus (Rom. 1:1). However, in this latter case the
servility and abjectness are not included in the meaning of
the word, but the fact that the Bible writers used it to describe
the Christian, shows that they desired to retain its connotation
of humbleness on the part of the slave. As bondslaves of the
Lord Jesus, we are to ever remember that we must serve Him
in all humility of mind. Using the various meanings of *doulos*,
the reader can see for himself how the classical usage of the
word is in exact accord with its doctrinal implications in the
N.T. For instance, a sinner is born into slavery to sin by his
physical birth, and into a loving servitude to the Lord Jesus
by his spiritual new-birth. *Doulos* is found in the following
places: *Mt.* 8:9, 10:24, 25, 13:27, 28, 18:23, 26, 27, 28, 32, 20:
27, 21:34, 35, 36, 22:3, 4, 6, 8, 10, 24:45, 46, 48, 50, 25:14, 19,
21, 23, 26, 30, 26:51; *Mk.* 10:44, 12:2, 4, 13:34; 14:47; *Lk.* 2:29,
7:2, 3, 8, 10, 12:37, 38, 43, 45, 46, 47, 14:17, 21, 22, 23, 15:22,
17:7, 9, 10, 19:13, 15, 17, 22, 20:10, 11, 22:50; *John* 4:51, 8:34,
35, 13:16, 15:15, 15:20, 18:10, 18, 26; *Acts* 2:18, 4:29, 16:
17; *Rom.* 1:1, 6:16, 17, 19, 20; *I Cor.* 7:21, 22, 23, 12:13; *II Cor.*
4:5; *Gal.* 1:10, 3:28, 4:1, 7; *Eph.* 6:5, 6, 8; *Phil.* 1:1, 2:7; *Col*
3:11, 22, 4:1, 12; *I Tim.* 6:1; *II Tim.* 2:24; *Tit.* 1:1, 2:9; *Phm.*
16, *Jas.* 1:1; *I Pet.* 2:16; *II Pet.* 1:1, 2:19; *Jude* 1; *Rev.* 1:1,
2:20, 6:15, 7:3, 10:7, 11:18, 13:16, 15:3, 19:2, 5, 18, 22:3, 6.
Doulos is translated in these passages by the words "servant,
bond, or bondman." The verb *douleuo* which has the same
root as *doulos,* having therefore the same implications, and
which means "to be a slave, to serve, to do service, to obey,
to submit to," in a good sense "to yield obedience to, to obey
one's commands and render to him the services due," is found
in *Acts* 7:6; *Rom.* 6:18, 22; *I Cor.* 7:15, 9:19; *Gal.* 4:3; *Tit.* 2:3;
II Pet. 2:19. It is translated either by the word "servant" or

"bondage," together with the accompanying verb, and in Tit. 2:3 by the word "given."

Our next word is *therapon*. Trench says of this word: "The *therapon* . . . is the performer of present services, with no respect to the fact whether as a freeman or slave he renders them; as bound by duty, or impelled by love; and thus, as will necessarily follow, there goes habitually with the word the sense of one whose services are tenderer, nobler, freer than those of the *doulos*. Thus Achilles styles Patroclus his *therapon* . . ., one whose service was not constrained, but the officious ministration of love; very much like that of the squire or page of the Middle Ages. In the verb *therapeuo* (to serve, do service, to heal, cure, restore to health), . . . as distinguished from *douleuo* . . ., the nobler and tenderer character of the service comes still more strongly out. It may be used of the physician's watchful tendance of the sick, man's service to God, and is beautifully applied by Xenophon . . . to the care which the gods have of men.

"It will follow that the author of the Epistle to the Hebrews, calling Moses a *therapon* in the house of God (3:5), implies that he occupied a more confidential position, that a freer service, a higher dignity was his, than that merely of a *doulos*, approaching more closely to that of an *oikonomos* (the manager of a household, a steward, a superintendent) in God's house; and, referring to Num. 12:6-8, we find, confirming this view, that an exceptional dignity is there ascribed to Moses, lifting him above other *doulos* of God . . . It would have been well if our Translators had seen some way to indicate the exceptional and more honorable title given to him who 'was faithful in all God's house'." *Therapon* occurs but once in the N.T., at Heb. 3:5.

The next word is *diakonos*. It is derived, Trench thinks, from the verb *dioko* meaning "to hasten after, to pursue." Trench in comparing this word with the two preceding, has the following to say; "The difference between *diakonos* on one side, and *doulos* and *therapon* on the other, is this—that *diakonos* represents the servant in his activity for the work; ... not in his relation, either servile, as that of the *doulos,* or more voluntary, as in the case of the *therapon, to a person.* The attendants at a feast, and this with no respect to their condition as free or servile, are *diakonos* (John 2:5, Mt. 22: 13, compare John 12:2). The importance of preserving the distinction between *doulos* and *diakonos* may be illustrated from the parable of the Marriage Supper (Mt. 22:2-14). In our Version the king's 'servants' bring in the invited guests (v. 3, 4, 8, 10). and his 'servants' are bidden to cast out that guest who was without a wedding garment (v. 13); but in the Greek, those, the bringers-in of the guests, are *doulos*: these, the fulfillers of the king's sentence, are *diakonos*—this distinction being a most real one, and belonging to the essentials of the parable; the *doulos* being *men,* the ambassadors of Christ, who invite their fellowmen into His kingdom now, the *diakonos angels,* who in all the judgment acts at the end of the world evermore appear as the executors of the Lord's will."

Thus, *diakonos* represents the servant in his activity for the work he is to do. It speaks of one who executes the commands of another, especially of a master. The word is found in *Mt.* 20:26, 22:13, 23:11; *Mk.* 9:35, 10:43; *John* 2:5, 9, 12:26; *Rom.* 13:4, 15:8, 16:1; *I Cor.* 3:5; *II Cor.* 3:6, 6:4, 11:15, 23; *Gal.* 2:17; *Eph.* 3:7, 6:21; *Phil.* 1:1; *Col.* 1:7, 23, 25, 4:7; *I Thes.* 3:2; *I Tim.* 3:8, 12, 4:6.

Diakonos is translated in these places "minister, servant, deacon." The verb *diakoneo* which is from the same root and which means "to be a servant, attendant, domestic, to serve, to wait upon, to minister to one, to wait at table and offer food and drink to guests, to supply food and the necessaries of life, render ministering offices to, to minister a thing to one, to serve one with or by supplying anything," is found in *Mt.* 4:11, 8:15, 20:28, 25:44, 27:55; *Mk.* 1:13, 31, 10:45, 15:

41; *Lk.* 4:39, 8:3, 10:40, 12:37, 17:8, 22:26, 27; *John* 12:2, 26; *Acts* 6:2, 19:22; *Rom.* 15:25; *II Cor.* 3:3, 8:19, 20; *I Tim.* 3:10, 13; *II Tim.* 1:18; *Phm.* 13; *Heb.* 6:10; *I Pet.* 1:12, 4:10, 11. *Diakoneo* is translated in these places "minister, serve, administer."

The word *diakonia* which has the same root as *diakonos* and means "service, ministering," used especially of those who execute commands, is found in *Lk.* 10:40; *Acts* 1:17, 25, 6:1, 4, 11:29, 12:25, 20:24, 21:19; *Rom.* 11:13, 12:7, 15:31; *I Cor.* 12:5, 16:15; *II Cor.* 3:7, 8, 9, 4:1, 5:18, 6:3, 8:4, 9:1, 12, 13, 11:8; *Eph.* 4:12; *Col.* 4:17; *I Tim.* 1:12; *II Tim.* 4:5, 11; *Heb.* 1:14; *Rev.* 2:19. *Diakonia* is translated in these places "ministry, serving, ministration, office, administration, service."

Oiketes is the next word which we will treat. This word has the same root as the Greek word for "house" (*oikos*). It designates a house-servant, one holding closer relations to the family than other slaves. Trench says of this word; "*Oiketes* is often used as equivalent to *doulos*. It certainly is so in *I Pet.* 2:18; and hardly otherwise on the three remaining occasions on which it occurs in the N.T., (Lk. 16:13; Acts 10:7; Rom. 14:4) ; nor does the LXX (Ex. 21:27; Deut. 6:21; Prov. 17:2) appear to recognize any distinction between them; the Apocrypha as little (Eccl. 10:25). At the same time *oiketes* ('domesticus') does not bring out and emphasize the servile relation so strongly as *doulos* does; rather contemplates that relation from a point of view calculated to mitigate, and which actually did tend very much to mitigate, its extreme severity. He is one of the household, of the 'family', in the older sense of this word; not indeed necessarily one born in the house; *oikogenes* (born in the house, home-bred, said of a slave) is the word for this in the LXX (Gen. 14:14, Eccl. 2:7) ."

Our last word is *huperetes*. Trench says of this word: "*Huperetes* . . . is a word drawn from military matters; he was originally a rower . . ., as distinguished from the soldier, on board a war-galley; then the performer of any strong and hard labor; then the subordinate official who waited to accomplish the behests of his superior, as the orderly who attends a commander in war . . .; the herald who carries solemn messages. . . . In this sense, as an inferior minister to perform certain defined functions for Paul and Barnabas, Mark was their *huperetes* (Acts 13:5) ; and in this official sense of lictor, apparitor, and the like, we find the word constantly, indeed predominantly used in the N.T. (Mt. 5:25; Lk. 4:20; John 7:32, 18:18; Acts 5:22). The mention by St. John of *doulos* and *huperetes* together (18:18) is alone sufficient to indicate that a difference is by him observed between them; from which difference it will follow that he who struck the Lord on the face (John 18:22) could not be, as some suggest, the same whose ear the Lord had just healed (Lk. 22:51), seeing that this was a *doulos,* that profane and petulant striker a *huperetes,* of the High Priest. The meanings of *diakonos* and *huperetes* are much more nearly allied; they do in fact continually run into one another, and there are innumerable occasions on which the words might be indifferently used; the more official character and functions of the *huperetes* is the point in which the distinction between them resides."

The word is found in the following places: *Mt.* 5:25, 26:58; *Mk.* 14:54, 65; *Lk.* 1:2, 4:20; *John* 7:32, 45, 46, 18:3, 12, 18, 22, 36, 19:6; *Acts* 5:22, 26, 13:5, 26:16; *I Cor.* 4:1. It is translated by the words "officer, servant, minister."

We will now place these words together in a brief summary, so that the reader can obtain a bird's-eye view of the same and thus see them more clearly by way of contrast.

Doulos, the most common word, and one that spoke of a slave in the most servile condition, is not a specialized word. The chief idea that it conveys is that the slave is bound to his master. He is in a condition of bondage. The word *doulos* comes from *deo* which means "to bind." A *doulos* was a person who was born into the condition of slavery, one who was in a permanent relationship to his master which only death could break, one whose will was swallowed up in the will of his master, one who served his master even to the extent that he disregarded his own interests.

Therapon lays the emphasis upon the fact that the person serving is a performer of present services, with no respect to the fact whether as a freeman or a slave he renders them, whether bound by duty or impelled by love. There goes habitually with the word the sense of one whose services are tenderer, nobler, freer than those of a *doulos*.

Diakonos speaks of the servant in his activity for the work, not in his relation, either servile, as that of a *doulos*, or more voluntary, as in the case of a *therapon*. The word speaks of one who executes the commands of another, especially, those of a master.

Oiketes designates a household slave, one holding closer relations to the family than other slaves. He is one of the household of the "family."

Huperetes emphasizes the official capacity of the servant. It designated the subordinate official who waited to accomplish the behests of his superior.

To narrow our definitions down even more, we could say that *doulos* is a slave in his servile relation to his master, *therapon,* a slave whose services are more tender, nobler, and freer, *diakonos,* a slave seen in his activity executing the commands of his master, *oiketes* a household slave, and *huperetes,* a slave holding a subordinate official position.

PROPHECY. This is the translation of the Greek word *propheteuo.* We cannot do better than quote Trench's comments on this word. His presentation is by way of contrast, showing the difference between *propheteuo* and *manteuomai,* both originally used in the pagan religions, the former taken over into the Christian system, the latter, because of its objectionable heathen features, rejected. Trench has the following to say: "*Propheteuo* is a word of constant occurrence in the N.T.; *manteuomai* occurs but once, namely at Acts 16:16; where, of the girl possessed with the 'spirit of divination,' or 'spirit of Apollo,' it is said that she 'brought her masters much gain by *soothsaying*' (*manteuomai*). The abstinence from the use of this word on all other occasions, and the use of it on this one, is very observable, furnishing a notable example of that religious instinct wherewith the inspired writers abstain from words, whose employment would tend to break down the distinction between heathenism and revealed religion. Thus *eudaimonia,* although from a heathen point of view a religious word, for it ascribes happiness to the favor of some deity, is yet never employed to express Christian blessedness; nor could it fitly have been employed, *daimon* (a god, goddess, used of individual gods), which supplies its base, involving polytheistic error. In like manner *arete* the standing word in heathen ethics for 'virtue,' is of very rarest occurrence in the N.T.; it is found but once in all the writings of St. Paul (Phil. 4:8); and where else (which is only in the Epistles of St. Peter), it is in quite different uses from those in which Aristotle employs it. In the same way *ethe,* which gives us 'ethics," occurs only on a single occasion, and, which indicates that its absence elsewhere is not accidental, this once is in a quotation from a heathen poet (I Cor. 15:33).

"In conformity with this same law of moral fitness in the admission and exclusion of words, we meet with *propheteuo* as the constant word in the N.T., to express the prophesying by the Spirit of God: while directly a sacred writer has need to make mention of the lying art of heathen divination, he employs this word no longer, but *manteuomai* (to divine, to deliver an oracle, to presage, forebode) in preference (cf. I Sam. 28:8; Deut. 18:10). What the essential difference between the two things, 'prophesying' and 'soothsaying,' . . . is, and why it was necessary to keep them distinct and apart by different terms used to designate the one and the other, we shall best understand when we have considered the etymology of one, at least, of the words. But first, it is almost needless at this day to warn against what was once a very common error, one in which many of the Fathers shared, . . . namely a taking of the *pro* in *propheteuo* and *prophetes* (prophet) as temporal, which it is not any more than in *prophasis* (a pretext), and finding as the primary meaning of the word, he who declares things *before* they come to pass. This *fore*telling or *fore*announcing may be, and often is, of the office of the prophet, but is not of the essence of that office; and this as little in sacred as in classical Greek. The *prophetes* (prophet) is the *out*speaker; he who speaks *out* the counsel of God with the clearness, energy and authority which spring from the consciousness of speaking in God's name, and having received a direct message from Him to deliver. Of course all this appears in weaker and indistincter form in classical Greek, the word never coming to its full rights until used of the prophets of the true God. . . . From signifying . . . the interpreter of the gods, or of God, the word abated a little of the dignity of its meaning, and *prophetes* (prophet) was no more than as interpreter in a more general sense; but still of the good and true. . . . But it needs not to follow further the history of the word, as it moves outside the circle of Revelation. Neither indeed does it fare otherwise within this circle. Of the *prophetes* (prophet) alike of the Old Testament and of the New we may with the same confidence affirm that he is not primarily, but only accidentally, one who foretells things future; being rather one who, having been taught of God, speaks out his will (Deut. 18:18; Isa. 1; Jer. 1; Ezek. 2; I Cor. 14:3).

"In *manteuomai* we are introduced into quite a different sphere of things. The word, connected with *mantis* (one who divines, a seer, a presager, a foreboder) is through it connected, as Plato has taught us, with *mania* (madness, frenzy) and *mainomai* (to rage, be furious, to be mad, to rave, especially with anger). It will follow from this, that it contains a reference to the tumult of the mind, the *fury*, the temporary *madness*, under which those were, who were supposed to be possessed by the god, during the time that they delivered their oracles; this mantic fury of theirs displaying itself in the eyes rolling, the lips foaming, the hair flying, as in other tokens of a more than natural agitation. It is quite possible that these symptoms were sometimes produced, as no doubt they were often aggravated, in the seers, Pythonesses, Sibyls, and the like, by the inhalation of earth-vapours, or by other artificial excitements. . . . Yet no one who believes that real spiritual forces underlie all forms of idolatry, but will acknowledge that there was often much more in these manifestations than mere trickeries and frauds; no one with any insight into the awful mystery of the false religions of the world, but will see in these symptoms the result of an actual relation in which these persons stood to a spiritual world — a spiritual world, it is true, which was not above them, but beneath.

"Revelation, on the other hand, knows nothing of this mantic fury, except to condemn it. 'The spirits of the prophets are subject to the prophets' (I Cor. 14:32). But then he (namely, the prophet) is *lifted above,* not *set beside,* his everyday self. It is not discord and disorder, but a higher harmony and a diviner order, which are introduced into his soul; so that he is not as one overborne in the region of his lower life by forces stronger than his own, by an insurrection from beneath: but his spirit is lifted out of that region into a clearer atmosphere, a diviner day, than any in which at other times it is permitted him to breathe. All that he before had still remains his, only purged, exalted, quickened by a power higher than his own, but yet not alien to his own; for man is most truly man when he is most filled with the fulness of

God. Even within the sphere of heathenism itself, the superior dignity of the *prophetes* (prophet) to the *mantis* (one who divines, a seer, a presager, a foreboder) was recognized; and recognized on these very grounds. Thus there is a well-known passage in the Timaeus of Plato . . ., where exactly for this reason, that the *mantis* is one in whom all discourse of reason is suspended, who, as the word itself implies, more or less *rages,* the line is drawn broadly and distinctly between him and the *prophetes* (prophet), the former being subordinated to the latter, and his utterances only allowed to pass after they have received the seal and approbation of the other. . . . The truth which the best heathen philosophy had a glimpse of here, was permanently embodied by the Christian Church in the fact that, while it assumed the *propheteuo* (to prophecy) to itself, it relegated the *manteuomai* (to divine) to that heathenism which it was about to displace and overthrow."

The words "prophecy" (the noun), "prophecy" (the verb), and "prophet" are all the translations in the N.T., of the same Greek word which we have been studying, so that what is true of the verb *propheteuo* is true of the related nouns.

HEBREW (*Hebraios*), JEW (*Ioudaios*), ISRAELITE (*Israelites*). Trench offers a comparative study of these three titles which is most illuminating. He says: "All these names are used to designate members of the elect family and chosen race; but they are very capable, as they are very well worthy, of being discriminated.

"*Hebraios* (Hebrew) claims to be first considered. It brings us back to a period earlier than any when one, and very much earlier than any when the other, of the titles we compare with it, were, or could have been, in existence, . . . this title containing allusion to the *passing over* of Abraham from the other side of Euphrates; who was, therefore, in the language of the Phoenician tribes among whom he came, 'Abraham

the Hebrew,' or *Ho perates* (the one who is from beyond) as
it is well given in the Septuagint (Gen. 14:13), being from
beyond (peran) the river. . . . The name, as thus explained,
is not one by which the chosen people know themselves, but
by which others know them; not one which they have taken,
but which others have imposed on them; and we find the use
of *Hebraios* through all the O.T., entirely consistent with this
explanation of its origin. In every case it is either a title by
which foreigners designate the chosen race (Gen. 39:14, 17;
41:12; Ex. 1:16, 19; I Sam. 4:6; 13:19; 29:3; Judith 12:11) ; or
by which they designate themselves to foreigners (Gen. 40:15;
Ex. 2:7; 3:18; 5:3; 9:1; Jon. 1:9); or by which they speak of
themselves in tacit opposition to other nations (Gen. 43:32;
Deut. 15:12; I Sam. 13:3; Jer. 34:9, 14) ; never, that is, without
such national antagonism, either latent or expressed.

"When, however, the name *Ioudaios* (Jew) arose, as it did
in the later periods of Jewish history (the precise epoch will
be presently considered), *Hebraios* modified its meaning.
Nothing is more frequent with words than to retire into
narrower limits, occupying a part only of some domain
whereof once they occupied the whole; when, through the
coming up of some new term, they are no longer needed in
all their former extent; and when at the same time, through
the unfolding of some new relation, they may profitably lend
themselves to the expressing of this new. It was exactly thus
with *Hebraios*. In the N.T., that point of view external to
the nation, which it once always implied, exists no longer;
neither is every member of the chosen family an *Hebraios*
now, but only those who, whether dwelling in Palestine or
elsewhere, have retained the sacred Hebrew tongue as their
native language; the true complement and antithesis to
Hebraios being *Hellenistes,* a word first appearing in the
N.T., . . . and there employed to designate a Jew of the Dis-
persion who has unlearned his proper language, and now

speaks Greek, and reads or hears read in the synagogue the Scriptures in the Septuagint Version.

"This distinction first appears in Acts 6:1, and is probably intended in the two other passages, where *Hebraios* occurs (II Cor. 11:22; Phil. 3:5); as well as in the superscription, on whosoever authority it rests, of the Epistle to the Hebrews. It is important to keep in mind that in language, not in place of habitation, lay the point of difference between the 'Hebrew' and the 'Hellenist.' He was a 'Hebrew,' wherever domiciled, who retained the use of the language of his fathers. Thus St. Paul, though settled in Tarsus, a Greek city in Asia Minor, describes himself as a 'Hebrew,' and of 'Hebrew' parents, 'a Hebrew of Hebrews' (Phil. 3:5; cf. Acts 23:6); though it is certainly possible that by all this he may mean no more than in a general way to set an emphasis on his Judaism. Doubtless, the greater number of 'Hebrews' *were* resident in Palestine; yet not this fact, but the language they spoke, constituted them such.

"It will be well however to keep in mind that this distinction and opposition of *Hebraios* to *Hellenistes* as a distinction *within the nation,* and not between it and other nations (which is clear at Acts 6:1, and probably is intended at Phil. 3:5; II Cor. 11:22), is exclusively a Scriptural one, being hardly recognized by later Christian writers, not at all by Jewish and heathen. . . . Only this much of it is recognized, that *Hebraios,* though otherwise a much rarer word than *Ioudaios* (Jew), is always employed when it is intended to designate the people *on the side of their language.* This rule Jewish, heathen, and Christian writers alike observe, and we speak to the present day of the *Jewish* nation, but of the *Hebrew* tongue.

"This name *Ioudaios* (Jew) is of much later origin. It does not carry us back to the very birth and cradle of the chosen people, to the day when the Father of the faithful passed over the river, and entered on the land of inheritance; but keeps

rather a lasting record of the period of national disruption
and decline. It arose, and could only have arisen, with the
separation of the tribes into the two rival kingdoms of Israel
and Judah. Then, inasmuch as the ten tribes, though with
worst right, . . . assumed Israel as a title to themselves, the two
drew their designation from the more important of them, and
of Judah came the name . . . *Ioudaios*. . . . We meet *Ioudaios*,
or rather its Hebrew equivalent, in books of the sacred canon
composed anterior to, or during, the Captivity, as a designation of those who pertained to the smaller section of the
tribes, to the kingdom of Judah (II Kin. 16:6; Jer. 32:12;
34:9; 38:19) ; and not first in Ezra, Nehemiah, and Esther;
however in these, and especially in Esther, it may be of far
more frequent occurrence.

"It is easy to see how the name extended to the whole nation. When the ten tribes were carried into Assyria, and were
absorbed and lost among the nations, that smaller section of
the people which remained henceforth represented the whole;
and thus it was only natural that *Ioudaios* should express,
as it now came to do, not one of the kingdom of Judah as
distinguished from that of Israel, but any member of the
nation, a 'Jew' in this wider sense, as opposed to a Gentile.
In fact, the word underwent a process exactly the converse of
that which *Hebraios* had undergone. For *Hebraios,* belonging first to the whole nation, came afterwards to belong to a
part only; while *Ioudaios,* designating at first only the member of a part, ended by designating the whole. It now, in its
later, like *Hebraios* in its earlier, stage of meaning, was a
a title by which the descendant of Abraham called himself,
when he would bring out the national distinction between
himself and other peoples (Rom. 2:9, 10) ; thus 'Jew and
Gentile;' never '*Israelite* and Gentile:' or which others used
about him, when they had in view this same fact; thus the
Eastern Wise Men inquire, 'Where is He that is born King
of the Jews' (Matt. 2:2) ? testifying by the form of this ques-

tion that they were themselves Gentiles, for they would certainly have asked for the King *of Israel,* had they meant to claim any nearer share in Him. So, too, the Roman soldiers and the Roman governor give to Jesus the mocking title, 'King of the Jews' (Matt. 27:29, 37), while his own countrymen, the high priests, challenge Him to prove by coming down from the cross that He is 'King *of Israel*' (Matt. 27:42).

"For indeed the absolute name, that which expressed the whole dignity and glory of a member of the theocratic nation, of the people in peculiar covenant with God, was *Israelites.* . . . This name was for the Jew his especial badge and title of honor. To be descendants of Abraham, this honor they must share with the Ishmaelites (Gen. 16:15); of Abraham and Isaac with the Edomites (Gen. 24:25); but none except themselves were the seed of Jacob, such as in this name of Israelite they were declared to be. Nor was this all, but more gloriously still, their descent was herein traced up to him, not as he was Jacob, but as he was Israel, who as a Prince had power with God and with men, and prevailed (Gen. 32:28). That this title was accounted the noblest, we have ample proof. Thus, as we have seen, when the ten tribes threw off their allegiance to the house of David, they claimed in their pride and pretension the name of 'the kingdom of *Israel*' for the new kingdom which they set up—the kingdom, as the name was intended to imply, in which the line of the promises, the true succession of the early patriarchs, ran. So, too, there is no nobler title with which the Lord can adorn Nathanael than that of 'an *Israelite* indeed' (John 1:47), one in whom all which that name involved might indeed be found. And when St. Peter, and again when St. Paul, would obtain a hearing from the men of their own nation, when therefore they address them with the name most welcome to their ears, *andres Israelitai* (men, Israelites) (Acts 2:22; 3:12; 13:16; cf. Rom. 9:4; Phil. 3:5; II Cor. 11:22) is still the language with which they seek to secure their good-will.

"When, then, we restrict ourselves to the employment in the N.T., of these three words, and to the distinctions proper to them there, we may say that *Hebraios* is a Hebrew-speaking as contrasted with a Greek-speaking, or Hellenizing, Jew (which last in our Version we have well called a 'Grecian,' as differenced from *Hellen,* a veritable 'Greek' or other Gentile) ; *Ioudaios* is a Jew in his national distinction from a Gentile; while *Israelites,* the augustest title of all, is a Jew as he is a member of the theocracy, and thus an heir of the promises. In the first is predominantly noted his language; in the second his nationality . . .; in the third his theocratic privileges and glorious vocation."

GRACE (*charis*), MERCY (*eleos*). Trench has the following to say about these important words; "There has often been occasion to observe the manner in which Greek words taken up into Christian use are glorified and transformed, seeming to have waited for this adoption of them, to come to their full rights, and to reveal all the depth and the riches of meaning which they contained, or might be made to contain. *Charis* is one of these. It is hardly too much to say that the Greek mind has in no word uttered itself and all that was at its heart more distinctly than in this; so that it will abundantly repay our pains to trace briefly the steps by which it came to its highest honors. *Charis* . . . is first of all that property in a thing which causes it to give joy to the hearers or beholders of it, . . . and then, seeing that to a Greek there was nothing so joy-inspiring as grace or beauty, it implied the presence of this. . . .

"But *charis* after a while came to signify not necessarily the grace or beauty of a thing, as a quality appertaining to it; but the gracious or beautiful thing, act, thought, speech, or person it might be, itself — the grace embodying and uttering itself, where there was room or call for this, in gracious outcomings toward such as might be its objects; not any longer

'favor' in the sense of beauty, but 'the favor'; for our word
here a little helps us to trace the history of the Greek. . . .
There is a further sense which the word obtained, namely the
thankfulness which the favor calls out in return; this also
frequent in the N.T., (Luke 17:9; Rom. 6:17; II Cor. 8:16;
though with it, as we are only treating the word in its relations to *eleos,* (mercy) we have nothing to do. It is at that
earlier point which we have just been fixing that *charis* waited
for and obtained its highest consecration; not indeed to have
its meaning changed, but to have that meaning ennobled,
glorified, lifted up from the setting forth of an earthly to the
setting forth of a heavenly benefit, from signifying the favor
and grace and goodness of man to man, to setting forth the
favor, grace and goodness of God to man, and thus, of necessity, of the worthy to the unworthy, of the holy to the sinful.
. . . Such was a meaning to which it had never raised itself
before, and this not even in the Greek Scriptures of the elder
Covenant. . . .

"Already, it is true, if not there, yet in another quarter
there were preparations for this glorification of meaning to
which *charis* was destined. These lay in the fact that already
in the ethical terminology of the Greek schools *charis* implied
ever a favor freely done, without claim or expectation of return — the word being thus predisposed to receive its new
emphasis, its religious, I may say its dogmatic, significance; to
set forth the entire and absolute freeness of the lovingkindness
of God to men. Thus Aristotle, defining *charis,* lays the
whole stress on this very point, that it is conferred freely, with
no expectation of return, and finding its only motive in the
bounty and free-heartedness of the giver. . . . St. Paul sets
charis and *erga* (works) over against one another in directest
antithesis, showing that they mutually exclude one another,
it being of the essence of whatever is owed to *charis* that it is
unearned and unmerited. . . .

"But while *charis* has thus reference to the *sins* of men, and is that glorious attribute of God which these sins call out and display, his free *gift* in their forgiveness, *eleos* (mercy) has special and immediate regard to the *misery* which is the consequence of these sins, being the tender sense of this misery displaying itself in the effort, which only the continued perverseness of man can hinder or defeat, to assuage and entirely remove it. . . . Of *eleos* we have this definition in Aristotle, "Mercy is a certain grief at that which is seen to be evil, pernicious, and wretched, to meet with that which is unworthy, that which he himself in fear expected that he might suffer, or certain of his own" (author's translation). It will be at once perceived that much will have here to be modified, and something removed, when we come to speak of the *eleos* of God. Grief does not and cannot touch Him, in whose presence is fulness of joy; He does not demand unworthy suffering, . . . which is the Stoic definition of *eleos* . . . to move Him, seeing that absolutely unworthy suffering there is none in a world of sinners; neither can He, who is lifted up above all chance and change, contemplate, in beholding misery, the possibility of being Himself involved in the same. . . . We may say then that the *charis* of God, his free grace and gift, displayed in the forgiveness of sins, is extended to men, as they are *guilty*, his *eleos*, as they are *miserable*. The lower creation may be, and is, the object of God's *eleos*, inasmuch as the burden of man's curse has redounded also upon it (Job 38:41; Ps. 147:9; John 4:11; Rom. 8:20-23), but of his *charis* man alone; he only needs, he only is capable of receiving it.

"In the Divine mind, and in the order of our salvation as conceived therein, the *eleos* precedes the *charis*. God so *loved* the world with a pitying love (herein was the *eleos*), that He *gave* his only begotten Son (herein the *charis*), that the world through Him might be saved (cf. Eph. 2:4; Luke 1:78, 79). But in the order of the manifestation of God's purposes of salvation the grace must go before the mercy, the *charis* must go before and make way for the *eleos*. It is true that the same persons are the subjects of both, being at once the guilty and the miserable; yet the righteousness of God, which it is quite as necessary should be maintained as his love, demands that the guilt should be done away, before the misery can be assuaged; only the forgiven may be blessed. He must pardon, before He can heal; men must be justified before they can be sanctified. And as the righteousness of God absolutely and in itself requires this, so no less that righteousness as it has expressed itself in the moral constitution of man, linking as it there has done misery with guilt, and making the first the inseparable companion of the second. From this it follows that in each of the apostolic salutations where these words occur, *charis* precedes *eleos* (I Tim. 1:2; II Tim. 1:2; Tit. 1:4; II John 3); nor could this order have been reversed. *Charis* on the same grounds in the more usual Pauline salutations precedes *eirene* (peace) (I Cor. 1:3; II Cor. 1:2); and often."

The word *charis* is rendered by the word "grace" in its every occurrence in the N.T., except in the following places: It has its purely classical meaning of the thankfulness which a favor calls out, in *Lk.* 6:32, 33, 34, 17:9; *Rom.* 6:17; *I Cor.* 15:57; *II Cor.* 2:14, 8:16, 9:15; *I Tim.* 1:12; *II Tim.* 1:3 (thanks). In I Pet 2:19, 20 (thankworthy, acceptable) we have an interesting use of the word. It means there "an action which is beyond the ordinary course of what is expected, and is therefore commendable." What a descriptive characterization of Calvary. *Charis* is translated "favor" in Lk. 1:30, 2:52; Acts 7:10, 46. One of the classical usages of *charis* was that of the favor with which the Greek would regard anything that was beautiful. That feeling of favor which the Greek had for something beautiful, included the element of pleasure which he derived from its contemplation, of being pleasantly disposed to that thing, of having admiration for it. *Charis* is used again in its purely classical usage in Lk. 4:22, where it is translated "gracious," and where it speaks of words full of beauty, of the pleasing properties of the words of the Lord Jesus, words which excited wonder, admiration, joy. *Charis* is translated "pleasure" in Acts 24:27, 25:9, where it refers to what the Jews would have considered a gracious act toward them, one they did not deserve, an act beyond the ordinary course of what might be expected. The word *charis* is translated "liberality" in I Cor. 16:3, where it refers to the money-gift which the Gentile Christians were sending to the Jewish Christians in Jerusalem. Surely, this gift from the natural standpoint was something beyond the ordinary course of what might be expected, and was therefore commendable. These Gentiles were former pagans with an antipathy towards the Jewish race. But the grace of God in them made them kindly disposed toward Jews whom they had never seen. *Charis* is translated "benefit" in II Cor. 1:15. Paul is speaking here about the spiritual benefits which the Corinthian Christians would receive from his teaching, should he come to them again. From the genius of the word *charis*, we would judge that the spiritual "benefit" they would receive, would be far in excess of what they deserved, and in character so rich that it would be received with great rejoicing. In Phm. 7, *charis* is translated "joy." Here we have another classical usage of the word. *Charis* is related to *chairo* which means "to rejoice, be glad, be delighted or pleased." Thus, the noun *charis* on occasion means "joy."

Cremer has some valuable material on *charis*. He says: "The import of this word has been in a peculiar manner determined and defined by the peculiar use of it in the N.T., and especially in the Pauline Epistles. We cannot affirm that its scriptural use seriously differs from or contradicts its meaning in the classics, for the elements of the conception expressed by it are only emphasized in a distinctive manner in Holy Scripture; but by this very means it has become quite a different word in N.T., Greek, so that we may say it depended upon Christianity to realize its full import, and to elevate it to its rightful sphere. It signifies in the N.T., what we designate *Gnade,* grace, a conception which was not expressed by *charis* in profane Greek, and which, indeed, the classics do not contain. It may be affirmed that this conception, to express which the Greek *charis* has been appropriated as a perfect synonym, — a conception in its distinctive compass quite different from the negative *to pardon, to remit,* — first appeared with, and was first introduced by, Christianity. . . . We may, perhaps, add that no language so fully and accurately presents a synonym for it as does Old High German 'ginada,' literally, 'a coming near,' or 'an inclining towards.' " . . . The English word *grace* corresponds fully with the German *Gnade.*

"Now *charis* . . . signifies a kind affectionate, pleasing nature, and inclining disposition either in person or thing. Objectively, and for the most part physically, it denotes personal gracefulness, a pleasing work, beauty of speech, . . . gracefulness, agreeableness. . . . Then subjectively it means an inclining towards, . . . courteous or gracious disposition, friendly willingness, both on the part of the giver and the receiver; in the former case, *kindness, favor;* in the latter, *thanks, respect,* homage; favor, kindness, inclination towards; the disposition as generally cherished and habitually manifested, and as shown in the bestowment of a favor or in a service of love to anyone. . . .

"But the word especially denotes God's grace and favor *towards mankind or to any individual,* which, as a free act, excludes merit, and is not hindered by guilt, but forgives sin; it thus stands out in contrast with *erga* (works), *nomos* (law), *hamartia* (sin). It is called grace as denoting the relation and conduct of God towards sinful man. . . .

"*Charis* has been distinctly appropriate in the N.T. to designate the relation and conduct of God towards sinful man as revealed in and through Christ, especially as an act of spontaneous favor, of favor wherein no mention can be made of obligation. . . . This element of spontaneousness is not prominent in the classical use of the word, though it is traceable even here. . . . But in the N.T. this element is specially emphasized. . . . With the worthlessness of works in connection with grace we thus have the non-imputation and forgiveness of sin, i.e., *apolutrosis* (a releasing effected by payment of a ransom), and as a *third* element, the positive gift of *dikaiosis* (righteousness), leading on to *zoe* (life). . . . Thus it must be recognized that the Greek word in its application attains for the first time an application and sphere of use adequate to its real meaning; previously it was like a worn-out coin. . . .

"It cannot be said, however, that the N.T. *charis* denotes 'a manifestation of grace' corresponding with the classical signification, *an act of kindness or of favor.* The distinction made between *charis* and *doron* (a gift) shows this, cf. Rom. 5:15, 'the grace of God and the gift by grace'. . . . So also *didonai charis* (to give grace), in Scripture, must not be confounded with the same expression in profane Greek, where it means *to perform an act of kindness;* in Scripture it signifies, *to give grace, to cause grace to be experienced. . . .*"

Comparing *charis* with *eleos,* Cremer has the following: "*Eleos,* though adopted into the N.T. treasury, leaves untouched an essential aspect of the scriptural or N.T. conception of grace, inasmuch as it is used to express *the divine behavior towards wretchedness and misery, not towards sin.* It is just this aspect — the relation of *grace* to sin — which must not be overlooked; in this freeness of grace — the *spontaneous inclination* which does not lie in *eleos* — is for the first time fully realized."

Charis is used in the N.T., of that spontaneous act of God that came from the infinite love in His heart, in which He stepped down from His judgment throne to take upon Himself the guilt and penalty of human sin, thus satisfying His justice, maintaining His government, and making possible the bestowal of salvation upon the sinner who receives it by faith in the Lord Jesus Christ who became a Sin-offering for him on the Cross (Rom. 3:24).

Charis also refers to the salvation which God provides, which salvation includes justificatidn, sanctification, and glorification (Tit. 2:11). In Rom. 3:24 it is justifying grace. In Eph. 1:2 it is sanctifying grace, the enabling grace of God in the operation of the Holy Spirit in the life of the yielded saint. See also II Cor. 12:9, 8:6, 7; Heb. 4:16, 12:28.

EMPTY (*kenos*), VAIN (*mataios*). Trench has the following on these words: "The first, *kenos,* is 'empty,' . . . the second, *mataios,* 'vain.' . . .In the first is characterized the hollowness, in the second the aimlessness, or, if we may use the word, the resultlessness, connected as it is with *maten* (in vain, idly, fruitlessly), of that to which this epithet is given. Thus *kenai elpides* are empty hopes, such as are built on no solid foundation; and in the N.T. *kenoi logoi* (Eph. 5:6; cf. Deut. 32:47; Ex. 5:9) are words which have no inner substance and kernel of truth, hollow sophistries and apologies for sin; *kenos kopos,* labor which yields no return (I Cor. 15:58) ; so *kenophoniai* (empty discussion, discussion of vain and empty matters) (I Tim. 6:20; II Tim. 2:16); . . . and *kenodoxia* (groundless self-esteem, empty pride) (Phil. 2:3). . . . St. Paul reminds the Thessalonians (I Thes. 2:1) that his entrance to them was not *kene* (empty, vain), not unaccompanied with the demonstration of Spirit and of power. When used not of things but of persons, *kenos* predicates not merely an absence and emptiness of good, but, since the moral nature of man endures no vacuum, the presence of evil. It is thus employed only once in the N.T., namely at Jas. 2:20, where the *kenos anthropos* (vain man) is one in whom the higher wisdom has found no entrance, but who is puffed up with a vain conceit of his own spiritual insight, *'aufgeblasen'* (puffed up), as Luther has it. . . .

"But if *kenos* thus expresses the emptiness of all which is not filled with God, *mataios* (vain), as observed already, will express the aimlessness, the leading to no object or end, the vanity, of all which has not Him, who is the only true object and end of any intelligent creature, for its scope. In things natural it is *mataios* (vain), as Gregory of Nyssa, in his first *Homily on Ecclesiastes* explains it, to build houses of sand on the sea-shore, to chase the wind, to shoot at the stars, to pursue one's own shadow. . . . That toil is *mataios* (vain) which can issue in nothing . . .; that grief is *mataios* (vain) for which no ground exists . . .; that is a *mataios euche* (a vain prayer, entreaty, wish or vow) which in the very nature of things cannot obtain its fulfilment . . .; the prophecies of the false prophet, which God will not bring to pass, are *manteiai mataiai* (vain prophesyings) (Ezek. 13:6, 7, 8); so in the N.T. *mataioi kai anopheleis zeteseis* (Tit. 3:9) are idle and unprofitable questions whose discussion can lead to no advancement in true godliness; cf. *mataiologia* (I Tim. 1:6) *mataiologoi* (Tit. 1:10), vain talkers, the talk of whose lips can tend only to poverty, or to worse (Isa. 32:6:LXX); *mataioponia* (Clement of Rome, 9), labor which in its very nature is in vain.

"*Mataiotes* (what is devoid of truth and appropriateness, perverseness, depravity) is a word altogether strange to profane Greek; one too to which the old heathen world, had it possessed it, could never have imparted that depth of meaning which in Scripture it has obtained. For indeed that heathen world was itself too deeply and hopelessly sunken in 'vanity' to be fully alive to the fact that it was sunken in it at all; was committed so far as to have lost all power to pronounce that judgment upon itself which in this word is pronounced upon it. One must, in part at least, have been delivered from the *mataiotes,* to be in a condition at all to esteem it for what it truly is. When the Preacher exclaimed 'All is vanity' (Eccl. 1:2), it is clear that something in him was *not* vanity, else he could never have arrived at this conclusion. . . . It is not too much to say that of one book in Scripture, I mean of course the book of The Preacher, it is the key-word. In that book *mataiotes,* or its Hebrew equivalent, . . . occurs nearly forty times; and this 'vanity,' after the preacher has counted and cast up the total good of man's life and labors apart from God, constitutes the zero at which the sum of all is rated by him. The false gods of heathendom are eminently *ta mataia* (the vain things) (Acts 14:15; cf. II Chron. 11:15; Jer. 10:15; John 2:8); the *mataiousthai* (the becoming vain) is ascribed to as many as become followers of these (Rom. 1:21; II Kin. 17:15; Jer. 2:5; 28:17, 18); inasmuch as they, following after vain things, become themselves *mataiophrones,* (3 Macc. 6:11), like the vain things which they follow (Wisd. 13:1; 14:21-31); their whole conversation vain (I Pet. 1:18), the *mataiotes* (the vanity) having reached to the very center and citadel of their moral being, to the *nous* (mind) itself (Eph. 4:17). Nor is this all; this *mataiotes,* or *douleia tes phthoras* (bondage of corruption) (Rom. 8:21), for the phrases are convertible, of which the end is death, reaches to that entire creation which was made dependant on man; and which with a certain blind consciousness of this is ever reaching out after a deliverance, such as it is never able to grasp, seeing that the restitution of all other things can only follow on the previous restitution of man."

But let us look at this word *mataios* again. Our word "vain" today usually means pride. It is so used once in the N.T. Thayer gives us further light on this word. He says it means, "devoid of force, truth, success, result, useless, to no purpose." Moulton and Milligan quote a clause from the papyri which perfectly illustrates the use of the word *mataios*: "wherein he vainly relates that he was ignorant of the securities which had been given him." They gave an illustration of the use of *mataiotes*: "suggests either absence of purpose or failure to attain any true purpose." Thus, these words refer to an ineffectual effort to attain some end or to the inability of something to function with respect to the purpose for which it is in existence or is intended. A vain religion is one which fails to measure up to what that life should be.

Regarding the word *kenos,* Thayer says: "empty, vain, devoid of truth; used metaphorically of endeavors, labors, acts, which result in nothing, it means vain, fruitless, without effect." It means "in vain, to no purpose." Moulton and Milligan give examples of its use in the papyri: "having rifled the contents aforesaid he threw the empty box into my house." They say that when applied to men as in Jas. 2:20 it means "pretentious, hollow." They quote another clause illustrating its use, "so that you shall oblige me to no purpose."

The reader will observe that *kenos* and *mataios* are very close together in their meanings, and that sometimes they can be used indiscriminately. But at times the distinction which Trench makes, still holds, namely, that *kenos* expresses the emptiness of all which is not filled with God, whereas *mataios* expresses the aimlessness, the leading to no object or end, the "in-vain-ness" of all that has not Him for its scope.

Kenos is found in *Mk.* 12:3; *Lk.* 1:53, 20:10, 11; Acts 4:25; *I Cor.* 15:10, 14, 58; *II Cor.* 6:1; *Gal.* 2:2; *Eph.* 5:6; *Phil* 2:16; *Col.* 2:8; *I Thes.* 2:1, 3:5; *Jas.* 2:20. It is translated in these places by the words "empty, vain."

Mataios occurs in *Acts* 14:15; *I Cor.* 3:20, 15:17; *Tit.* 3:9; *Jas.* 1:26; *I Pet.* 1:18. *Mataiotes* is found in *Rom.* 8:20; *Eph.* 4:17; *II Pet.* 2:18. The words "vanity" and "vain" appear in the translation. *Maten* is found in Mt. 15:9; Mk. 7:7. The translation is "in vain."

ANOTHER. This is the translation of *allos* and *heteros.* Trench says; "*Allos* is the numerically distinct; thus Christ spoke we are told 'another' parable, and still 'another,' but each succeeding one being of the same character as those

which He had spoken before (Matt. 13:23, 24, 31, 33), *allos*[34]
therefore in every case. But *heteros*, . . . superadds the notion
of qualitative difference. One is 'divers,' the other is 'diverse.'
There are not a few passages in the N.T. whose right interpretation, or at any rate their full understanding, will depend
on an accurate seizing of the distinction between these words.
Thus Christ promises to his disciples that He will send, not
heteros, but *allos*, *Parakleton* (John 14:16), 'another' Comforter therefore, similar to Himself. . . .

"But if in the *allos* there is a negation of identity, there is
oftentimes much more in *heteros*, the negation namely, up to
a certain point, of resemblance; the assertion not merely of
distinctness but of difference. A few examples will illustrate
this. Thus St. Paul says, 'I see another law' (*heteros nomos*),
a law quite different from the law of the spirit of life, even
a law of sin and death, 'working in my members' (Rom. 7:23).
After Joseph's death 'another king arose' in Egypt (*heteros
basileus*, Acts 7:18; cf. Ex. 1:8), one, it is generally supposed,
of quite another dynasty, at all events of quite another spirit,
from his who had invited the children of Israel into Egypt,
and so hospitably entertained them there. The *heteros hodos*
and *heteros kardia* which God promises that He will give to
his people are a new way and a new heart (Jer. 39:39; cf.
Deut. 29:22). It was not 'another spirit' only but a different
(*heteros pneuma*) which was in Caleb, as distinguished from
the other spies (Num. 14:24). In the parable of the Pounds
the slothful servant is *heteros* (Luke 19:18). . . . The spirit
that has been wandering through dry places, seeking rest in
them in vain, takes 'seven other spirits' (*heteros pneuma*),
worse than himself, of a deeper malignity, with whose aid to
repossess the house which he has quitted for a while (Matt.
12:45). Those who are crucified with the Lord are *heteros*

---

34. The Greek student will observe that the writer has kept *allos* and
heteros uniform without respect to their syntactical relations, for the
benefit of the English reader.

duo, kakourgoi, 'two others, madefactors,' as it should be
pointed (Luke 23:32) ; it would be inconceivable and revolt-
ing so to confound Him and them as to speak of them as
allos duo. It is only too plain why St. Jude should speak of
heteros sarx (different kind of flesh v. 7), as that which the
wicked whom he is denouncing followed after (Gen. 19:5).
Christ appears to his disciples *en heteros morphe* (in a different form) (Mark 16:12), the word indicating the mighty
change which had passed upon Him at his resurrection, as by
anticipation at his Transfiguration, and there expressed in
the same way (Luke 9:29). It is *heteros cheilesin,* with altogether other and different lips, that God will speak to his
people in the New Covenant (I Cor. 14:21) ; even as the
tongues of Pentecost are *heteros glossai* (Acts 2:4), being
quite different in kind from any other speech of men. It
would be easy to multiply the passages where *heteros* could
not be exchanged at all, or could only be exchanged at a loss,
for *allos,* at Matt. 11:3; I Cor. 15:40; Gal. 1:6. Others too
there are where at first sight *allos* seems quite as fit or a fitter
word; where yet *heteros* retains its proper force. Thus at
Luke 22:65 the *heteros polla* are . . . blasphemous speeches
now of one kind, now of another; the Roman soldiers taunt-
ing the Lord now from their own point of view, as a pretender
to Caesar's throne; and now from the Jewish, as claiming to
be Son of God. At the same time it would be idle to look for
qualitative difference as intended in every case where *heteros*
is used; thus see Heb. 11:36, where it would be difficult to
trace anything of the kind. . . .

"What holds good of *heteros,* holds good also of the com-
pounds into which it enters, of which the N.T. contains three;
namely, *heteroglossos* (I Cor. 14:21), by which word the
Apostle intends to bring out the non-intelligibility of the
tongues to many in the Church; it is true indeed that we have
also *alloglossos* (Ezek. 3:6) ; *heterodidaskalein* (I Tim. 1:3),
to teach other things, and things alien to the faith; *hetero-*

zugein (II Cor. 6:14), to yoke with others, and those as little to be yoked with as the ox with the ass (Deut. 22:10) . . . . So too we have in ecclesiastical Greek *heterodoxia,* which is not merely another opinion, but one which, in so far as it is another, is a worse, a departure from the faith. The same reappears in our own 'heterogeneous,' which is not merely of another kind, but of another and a worse kind. For this point deserves attention, and is illustrated by several of the examples already adduced; namely, that *heteros* is very constantly, not this other and different, *allos kai diaphoron,* only, but such with the farther subaudition, that whatever difference there is, it is for the worse. Thus Socrates is accused of introducing into Athens *heteros kaina daimonia* (different, evil, and new deities); *heteros daimon* is an evil or hostile deity; *heteros thusiai,* ill-omened sacrifices, such as bring back on their offerer not a blessing but a curse; *heteros demagogoi* are popular leaders not of a different only, but of a worse stamp and spirit than was Pericles. So too in the Septuagint other gods than the true are invariably *heteros theos* (Deut. 5:7; Judg. 10:13; Ezek. 42:18; and often). . . . A barbarous tongue is *heteros glossa* (Isa. 28:11) (a different kind of tongue) . . . .

"We may bring this distinction practically to bear on the interpretation of the N.T. There is only one way in which the fine distinction between *heteros* and *allos,* and the point which St. Paul makes as he sets the one over against the other at Gal. 1:6, 7, can be reproduced for the English reader. 'I marvel,' says the Apostle, 'that ye are so soon removed from them that called you into the grace of Christ unto *another* (*heteros*) Gospel, which is not *another*' (*allos*). Dean Alford for the first 'other' has substituted 'different'; for indeed that is what St. Paul intends to express, namely, his wonder that they should have so soon accepted a Gospel different in character and kind from that which they had already received, which therefore had no right to be called another Gospel, to assume this name, being in fact no Gospel at all; since there could not be two Gospels, varying the one from the other....

"There are other passages in the N.T. where the student may profitably exercise himself with the enquiry why one of these words is used in preference to the other, or rather why both are used, the one alternating with, or giving partial place to, the other. Such are I Cor. 12:8-10; II Cor. 11:4; Acts 4:12."

In summing up the difference between these two words we offer the following: *Heteros* means "another of a different kind," *allos*, "another of the same kind." *Heteros* denotes qualitative difference, *allos*, numerical difference. *Heteros* distinguishes one of two. *Allos* adds one besides. Every *heteros* is an *allos*, but not every *allos* is a *heteros*. *Heteros* involves the idea of difference, while *allos* denotes simply distinction of individuals. *Heteros* sometimes refers not only to difference in kind but also speaks of the fact that the character of the thing is evil or bad. That is, the fact that something differs in kind from something else, makes that thing sometimes to be of an evil character.

As an illustration of the importance of noting the distinction between these words when studying the N.T., we note that *heteros* in Mt. 11:3 solves the problem as to why John the Baptist came to doubt the Messiahship of the Lord Jesus. His question was, "Art thou He that should come, or look we for another (Messiah) of a different kind?" The Messiahship of the Lord Jesus had been authenticated to John at the former's baptism in Jordan, when the Father's voice from heaven said, "This is my beloved Son, in whom I am well pleased" (Mt. 3:17). He had announced Him both as Messiah (Mt. 3:1-3), and as the Lamb of God (John 1:36), or, in other words, as the King of Israel and the Saviour. In his preaching, John had in addition to this announced Jesus as a Messiah of Judgment (Mt. 3:11-12). But our Lord's ministry until His final rejection by official Israel had been as a Messiah of mercy, one who healed the sick, raised the dead, and forgave sins. The Lord Jesus as Messiah did not fit the picture that John had painted. John knew that his message had come from God. And since Jesus did not fit that picture of a Messiah of judgment, he questioned His Messiahship, and asked if he should look for a Messiah of a different (*heteros*) kind. Had John been alive when Jesus gave Jerusalem and the nation Israel over to judgment, and turned from the city and nation that rejected Him, the picture he painted would have been realized.

Heteros is found in the following places: *Mt.* 6:24, 8:21, 11:3, 12:45, 15:30, 16:14; *Mk.* 16:12; *Lk.* 3:18, 4:43, 5:7, 6:6, 7:41, 8:3, 6, 7, 8, 9:29, 56, 59, 61, 10:1, 11:16, 26, 14:19, 20, 31, 16:7, 13, 18, 17:34, 35, 18:10, 19:20, 20:11, 22:58, 65, 23:32, 40; *John* 19:37; *Acts* 1:20, 2:4, 13, 40, 4:12, 7:18, 8:34, 12:17, 13:35, 15:35, 17:7, 21, 34, 19:39, 20:15, 23:6, 27:1, 3; *Rom.* 2:1, 21, 7:3, 4, 23, 8:39, 13:8, 9; *I Cor.* 3:4, 4:6, 6:1, 8:4, 10:24, 29, 12:9, 10, 14:17, 21, 15:40; *II Cor.* 8:8, 11:4; *Gal.* 1:6, 19, 6:4; *Eph.* 3:5; *Phil* 2:4; *I Tim.* 1:10; *II Tim.* 2:2; *Heb.* 5:6, 7:11, 13, 15, 11:36; *Jas.* 2:25, 4:12; *Jude* 7. It is translated by the words "other, another, some, altered, else, next, one, strange." For instance, in Lk. 8:6, it is, "some of a different kind fell upon a rock." In Acts 17:21, the Athenians spent their time in nothing else of a different nature, showing how obsessed they were with the quest for something newer (the comparative is used in the Greek text). The minute they learned something new, it was toyed with as a novelty for a short while, then flung over the shoulder, and the quest for something newer was commenced again. In Jude 7, the fallen angels went after strange flesh, that is, flesh of a different nature and order of being than theirs, human flesh. Study the other places listed, and see how much additional light is thrown upon the English text.

The other word *allos,* is found so often in the N.T., that we cannot list its occurrences here. The student can check with the list of places where *heteros* is found. If the scripture location is not found there, *allos* appears in the Greek text.

FIGHT. This and other English words to be noted later, is the translation of *agonizomai* and the noun of the same root *agon*, both of which speak of great intensity of purpose and effort.

Agonizomai was a term used in Greek athletics. It meant "to contend for victory in the public athletic games, to wrestle as in a prize contest, straining every nerve to the uttermost towards the goal." *Agon* is the noun which speaks of the conflict or contest itself. The first-century Roman world was acquainted with these Greek athletic terms, for the Greek stadium was a familiar sight, and the Greek athletic games were well known in the large cities of the Empire. The Bible writers seized upon these terms, and used them to illustrate in a most vivid manner, the intensity of purpose and activity that should characterize both Christian living and Christian service. The present day football game is a fair example of the terrific struggle for supremacy in the Greek athletic games that was commonly seen by the first-century stadium crowds. The point is that if we Christians would live our Christian lives and serve the Lord Jesus with the intensity of purpose and effort that is put forth in a football contest, what God-glorifying lives we would live.

Agonizomai is used in *Lk.* 13:24; *John* 18:36; *I Cor.* 9:25; *Col.* 1:29, 4:12; *I Tim.* 6:12; *II Tim.* 4:7. It is translated by the words "strive, fight, labor fervently." *Agon* is found in *Phil.* 1:30; *Col.* 2:1; *I Thes.* 2:2; *I Tim.* 6:12; *II Tim.* 4:7; *Heb.* 12:1. The English words do not give us any idea of the intensity of purpose and effort that is found in the Greek words. Study these passages in the light of the meaning of the Greek text.

The word *agonia* is used in Lk. 22:44 where we have the words, "And being in an agony He prayed more earnestly."

Agonia speaks of combat, giving prominence to the pain and labor of the conflict. It is used in classical Greek, of fear, the emotion of a wrestler before the contest begins. It is not the same as *phobos* (fear), but trembling and anxiety about the issue. It speaks not of the fear that shrinks and would flee, but the fear that trembles as to the issue, an emotion which spurs on to the uttermost. This agony of soul was our Lord's in Gethsemane.

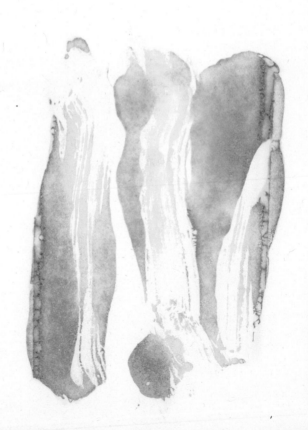